"When the Welfare People Come"

"When the Welfare People Come"

RACE AND CLASS
IN THE US CHILD PROTECTION SYSTEM

Don Lash

Haymarket Books
Chicago, Illinois

Published in 2017 by
Haymarket Books
P.O. Box 180165
Chicago, IL 60618
773-583-7884
www.haymarketbooks.org
info@haymarketbooks.org

ISBN: 978-1-60846-743-3

Distributed to the trade in the US through Consortium Book Sales and
Distribution (www.cbsd.com) and internationally through Ingram
Publisher Services International (www.ingramcontent.com).

This book was published with the generous support of Lannan
Foundation and Wallace Action Fund.

Special discounts are available for bulk purchases by organizations and
institutions. Please call 773-583-7884 or email info@haymarketbooks.org
for more information.

Cover design by Jamie Kerry of Belle Étoile Studios.

Printed in the United States.

Library of Congress Cataloging-in-Publication data is available.

10 9 8 7 6 5 4 3 2

CONTENTS

Introduction   1

1. The "Orphan Trains"—Then and Now   19

2. Moving Toward a Racialized Child Welfare System   31

3. Parents with Disabilities   59

4. Foster Youth   77

5. Foster Parents   99

6. Juvenile "Justice"   107

7. Toiling Inside the Bureaucracy   117

8. The Future of Child Welfare?   143

9. Real Reform   153

10. Child Welfare and Social Reproduction   169

11. Socialism and the Parent-Child Relationship   179

Acknowledgments   189

Appendix: From Rights to Reality—a Plan for Parent
Advocacy and Family-Centered Child Welfare Reform   193

Notes   195

Index   211

Introduction

In 2013, I was working for the New York City Administration for Children's Services (ACS), as an attorney specializing in education law. I was part of a unit charged with improving educational outcomes for children involved with ACS, although this often meant trying to make sure ACS involvement didn't disrupt or interfere with a child's school placement or services, on the principle of "first, do no harm." One morning, I represented my unit at "ChildStat," a weekly meeting presided over by ACS's commissioner, which was central to ACS's vision of accountability within the system under Mayor Michael Bloomberg. ChildStat was inspired by "ComStat," the much-hyped sessions started by the New York Police Department in the 1990s to review crime data at the precinct level and have the precinct commanders defend their data to the assembled brass. Under Bloomberg, the data-driven management review process spread to most other city agencies, including ACS. The ChildStat meeting was held in a custom-built amphitheater at ACS headquarters, featuring a raised dais for the people being grilled and terraced seats and desks with built-in microphones for the attendees. Brightly colored bar charts would flash by on multiple screens. This particular morning, the unit being reviewed was one of the field offices of the Division of Child Protection (DCP). Every neighborhood in the city is covered by one of these field offices, and it is a child protection specialist (CPS) from the appropriate field office who will be assigned to investigate an allegation of abuse or neglect called into the state central hotline. The DCP ChildStat sessions consisted of two parts. The first was a review of bar charts and tables showing caseloads, investigative time frames, and so on. The second part consisted of a review of three cases selected at random a few days before the meeting. For the case review, the managers were replaced on the dais by rank-and-file CPSs and mid-level supervisors. A summary without names or identifying details was prepared and distributed to all attendees. Official policy was that workers would face no consequence for deficiencies in performance identified during ChildStat, but it was still a grueling ordeal.

At this review, one of the cases was an allegation of physical abuse of an African American infant about three months old called in against her mother. The mother and baby were homeless and had been staying with a relative in public housing. One day, two people from the New York City Housing Authority (NYCHA) knocked at the door to check out the household composition. The mother, who was not on the lease, reported later that they demanded identification, and that she had to dress the baby and put her down in order to locate her ID and answer the questions. She said the visitors were impatient and kept pressuring her to hurry. One of the NYCHA people claimed that he witnessed the mother "throwing" the baby down onto a bare mattress on the floor. She acknowledged that she was flustered and anxious but denied throwing the baby and said the baby was not injured or hurt in any way. The CPS assigned to investigate the mother found her credible but asked her to take the child to an emergency room to be checked out. The child was examined and found to be healthy and well cared for, with no sign of injuries, and the CPS observed the mother to be a competent and loving caretaker. So the CPS believed the allegation of physical abuse should be considered "unfounded," but she and her supervisors hesitated to close the case because of concerns about the baby's living situation—specifically being homeless and doubled up, and sleeping on a mattress on the floor. There was also a concern that once the mother left the apartment she was in, she would have nowhere else to go. Her only other relative in the city was a sister, and the CPS had learned that some years previously, when the mother was a teenager, her sister had been arrested for attacking her with a knife. While the initial allegation was no longer an issue, CPS felt it could not close the case because of the lack of housing options and money to buy a proper crib, as well as the mom's past status as a victim of domestic violence. While the last issue was mentioned in part as evidence that the sister was not a viable housing resource, there also seemed to be a suggestion that, because she had been the victim of domestic violence as a teenager, the mother might be prone to unstable family relationships.

I don't know what happened to this parent and child, although I'd guess that the case was closed as unfounded within the sixty-day time frame allocated for investigations. There seemed to be no support for removing the child or forcing the mother to accept services (which wouldn't have addressed the core economic needs of the family in any event). I include the story because it illustrates some of the features of the child welfare system that will be discussed in the pages to follow.

This family's biggest problem was poverty, and the mother's experience with ACS did nothing to change that. None of the attendees of ChildStat that morning, from the commissioner on down, could offer any suggestions that would make stable, affordable housing or adequate income available to this mother and baby.

This mother was vulnerable to being accused of abuse or neglect because she was poor, which meant that she was subject to scrutiny and investigation by the housing authority. She almost certainly interacts with other agencies that monitor poor families, including welfare and public hospitals. Once the allegation was made, the focus shifted rapidly from the initial allegation to every aspect of this mother's life and past, and her "case"—with the threat of losing her child—was being kept open because she didn't have the money to secure an apartment and buy a crib. If the case was "indicated" (meaning that the CPS felt abuse or neglect was probable), not only would removal of the child be a real possibility, but the mother would also be barred from whole categories of future employment, in day care, schools, health care, elder care, in-home personal care, and so on. If she was previously unaware of the power ACS could wield over her family and future—which is unlikely given that she lived in a neighborhood in which everyone tends to be keenly aware of ACS—she is no doubt very conscious of the threat now, even if in the end ACS took no action against her.

There was no evident personal animosity or class bias toward the mother from the DCP workers. All were working-class women of color with extensive knowledge of the communities within which they conducted investigations. They were skeptical of the allegations from NYCHA, and credited the mother with being a very good caretaker. They also seemed to understand that the mother's housing problem was beyond her control. Nevertheless, they had been taught to identify "risk factors," including past family conflict, and to hold the mother responsible, as the only person over whom they had power, for anything that potentially threatened her child. The system and what they had been taught about case practice gave them no other alternatives.

Anatomy of the Child Welfare System

When we refer to the "child welfare system," we are talking about a massive network of public and private entities charged with responsibility in various ways for child safety and well-being. State and local agencies, nonprofit organizations, for-profit companies,[1] special courts, placement facilities, and foster homes are among the entities wholly dedicated to the system. Schools, childcare agencies, health care providers, and police also function as components of the system. The provision of "out-of-home care" (foster care) is the most extreme, coercive manifestation of the child welfare system, which consists of a range of interventions backed by the implicit or explicit threat of removal to out-of-home care. We can summarize the functions of various components of the system as follows: public outreach campaigns, voluntary services, training and policing of "mandated reporters" of abuse and neglect in various community institutions, child protective investigation of allegations of abuse and neglect, mandated services, foster care, and adoption. I will argue that the juvenile justice system should properly be viewed as overlapping both the child welfare and criminal justice systems, and in many ways as a bridge between the two.

Currently, the foster care system in the United States houses about four hundred thousand children. Children and youth flow into and out of the system, with a substantial percentage returning home, being adopted, or "aging out" each year, and a comparable percentage entering care. About half the children in foster care are housed with non-relative foster parents, another quarter with relatives ("kinship" foster parents), and the remainder in group homes, residential treatment, or on "trial discharge" to their birth parents while still legally in care.[2]

The child welfare system casts an even larger shadow. For every removal from a parent and placement into foster care, there have been a much larger number of child welfare investigations to determine whether removal is necessary. In New York City, the nation's largest municipal child welfare system, there were some 60,000 allegations in 2009 involving 90,000 children and youth, with 7,400 admitted into care and a total foster care population of 16,400.[3] The number of children impacted by the system during that year was therefore more than five times larger than the foster care population.

To varying degrees, this large population of children and families is subject to control and regulation. Parents of children in foster care are monitored by social workers, attorneys, and judges in family court (sometimes called "dependency court") proceedings, while countless others are subject to intrusive investigations under threat of removal. Often, removal is avoided through diversion into "family preservation" (defined by the federal government as "short-term, family-focused services designed to assist families in crisis by improving parenting and family functioning while keeping children safe") or "preventive" (defined as "strengthening protective factors for families and communities" to prevent child maltreatment) services, including mental health, domestic violence, and substance abuse services. The family may well be in need of such services, but is subject to extensive oversight from professionals with the potential to escalate child welfare involvement to coercive interventions if they believe, based on professional assessment and oversight, that parents are not complying with the demands of the system. In communities in which the child welfare system is most visible—generally poor and nonwhite—even families that never come into direct contact with it are aware that contact with the system may be triggered at any time by an injury to a child, a late pickup from childcare, or a dispute with a vengeful neighbor. Contact with the system may or may not result in an investigation, but serves as a reminder that the potential for intervention exists. Middle-class and affluent parents rarely receive such reminders, so for them the system is much more of an abstraction.

Child welfare involvement in the United States has always been associated with the children of the poor. In Wisconsin in 2008, for example, a child living in a home with less than $15,000 in household income was six times as likely to be involved with the system as a child from a home with a higher household income.[4] The poor are subject to greater scrutiny as a result of involvement with police, the welfare bureaucracy, homeless and public housing systems, publicly funded day care, and emergency rooms. Professionals who report allegations of abuse and neglect in schools, hospitals, and other social service facilities are most vigilant when interacting with low-income parents.[5] The reasons for this heightened vigilance are complex. Sometimes professionals consciously or unconsciously buy in to stereotypes about poor parents, especially Black parents, as more likely to be negligent or abusive than more affluent white parents who appear more like the supposed ideal of the nuclear family.[6] It would be unrealistic to expect that health care, school, and social welfare workers are completely immune to the coded racist attacks on "welfare mothers" and the media narrative about a "cycle of poverty."

It would be an even greater mistake to focus primarily on the personal beliefs of workers in these systems as responsible for the difference in the way systems interact with parents in poor non-white neighborhoods and in whiter, more affluent neighborhoods. Families in poor neighborhoods face complex problems of homelessness or housing insecurity, lack of money for food and other necessities, lack of childcare, and other issues that seldom threaten children in more affluent neighborhoods. And just like the DCP workers at ChildStat, workers in the system may see no other way of protecting children than by holding parents responsible for the poverty their children are living in. Additionally, parents with problems like domestic violence, drug or alcohol addiction, or who are in need of mental health treatment will have more options if they have good health insurance and the means to arrange childcare and take medical leave to obtain treatment, or to secure housing and escape an abusive relationship. Parents with fewer options are more likely to end up with child welfare involvement.

Equally important, the institutions employing these workers may enforce expectations that are different in poor neighborhoods. I am married to a school social worker working with mostly low-income parents in the Bronx. In a prior school, she was often instructed to make what she considered frivolous—or at the very least grossly premature—calls to the state hotline over things like a child coming to school with clothing that looked dirty, wearing an unseasonably light jacket, or with an unexplained injury that could be the result of a routine childhood mishap. She would sometimes finesse the situation to avoid making the call until she could talk to the parent, or she would make the call in such a way that the hotline operator would almost certainly not accept the allegation, but she could never completely disregard the "better safe than sorry" instinct of the school administrators to protect the institution by calling first and asking questions later.

The financing of the foster care system is complex, with a portion of each state's cost being reimbursed by the federal government at a rate that varies from state to state. Because of arcane eligibility rules, moreover, not all children qualify for federal reimbursement at the same rate, so quantifying the total cost of the system from all state and federal sources is difficult. By one estimate, the federal government spends about $9 billion a year on foster care, with states contributing at least as much.[7] Total child welfare cost, moreover, would include the cost of the reporting, investigative and court systems, adoption subsidies, and preventive services.

Capitalism and Child Welfare

In the United States, on which this book will focus, and in Western Europe, the system is and always has involved social control exercised over the children of the poorest segments of the working class. Among its primary purposes has been to prevent "these dangerous classes"—in the words of Charles Loring Brace, one of its earliest architects—from exploding in rage against the rule of capital.

I will argue that a related purpose has been supporting what Karl Marx described as the "perpetuation of labor power," by regulating and repairing families ravaged by poverty, discrimination, and attendant problems related to substance abuse, domestic violence, and mental health, to ensure the replacement in the workforce of parents by children. Marx and Engels showed that the primary role of the nuclear family for capital is to raise the next generation of workers. Real or perceived dysfunction in working-class families reduces the supply of labor power and raises the threat of a disruptive class. The modern child welfare system didn't exist in the time of Marx and Engels, and they never discussed the type of interventions into family life by the state for which child welfare institutions were created, but I believe that the Marxist understanding of "social reproduction," the role of the family in raising the next generation of the labor force, is important in providing an underlying justification for regulation of poor and working-class families. I also think it complements and enriches the framework of "stratified reproduction," which other writers in the field have used to explain the way in which parents who seemingly present as closer to a middle-class ideal are regarded as worthy of support and empowerment, while poor parents are regarded as suspect, especially if they are nonwhite.[8] While stratified reproduction helps to explain the ideology that has developed to make the regulation of poor families seem appropriate and normal, the Marxist notion of social reproduction, as sketched out by Marx and Engels and developed by more contemporary theorists such as Lise Vogel, is essential to understanding why capitalism needs to regulate poor and working-class families, and therefore why it needs an ideological framework to justify that.

Finally, the system performs important ideological functions for US capitalism. The United States has a higher rate of childhood poverty—more than one in five—than any other nation with an advanced economy, and ranked thirty-four out of thirty-five nations—edged out by Romania for last place—surveyed in 2013 by UNICEF.[9] Yet, the child welfare system helps to make the impoverishment and societal neglect of children tolerable to the larger population by promoting the idea that children are valued and protected. Perhaps of even greater importance, the system situates blame for the danger and harm imposed on children on their families rather than on the material conditions of their existence.

Serious maltreatment of children by parents and family caregivers certainly occurs, and many children who come into contact with the system have been physically, emotionally, or sexually abused. Others have experienced extreme neglect. Thus, child welfare intervention is necessary in many of the cases in which it occurs. Those who work within the system—as mandated reporters, child protective workers, social workers, lawyers, or clinicians—do not often have the luxury of reflecting on the relationship of capitalism to poverty, domestic violence, substance abuse and alcoholism, and child maltreatment. Confronted with a child in jeopardy, or a child who has experienced abuse or abandonment, workers must respond to the immediate threats, even if the underlying, overriding threat is capitalism itself.

This book is not intended to denigrate the efforts or the perceptions of workers who dedicate their careers to the protection of children. It is, rather, an invitation to those working within the system in whatever capacity to think critically about the system and their roles in its operation, and to think about the nature of reform in the short term and more transformative change in the long term.

The size and scope of the system is a product of the societal neglect that allows a nation with an extraordinarily advanced economy to relegate 20 percent of its children to poverty. Children who come to the attention of the system include those who are identified because of homelessness or housing insecurity and inadequate income to meet material needs. They also include those who experience abuse or neglect made more likely by overcrowded living conditions, lack of childcare, barriers to a mother escaping an abusive relationship, and lack of effective treatment for mental illness or substance abuse. The questions for those who work within the system are first: What kind of changes in child welfare services would make them less punitive and discriminatory toward those who are subject to intervention? What kind of changes in society would reduce the demand for child welfare services? And finally, how can families be supported in ways that don't threaten or stigmatize them?

The challenge for workers within the system is to recognize that fundamental change won't come through increased funding for the services they provide—although increased resources and resistance to austerity and privatization may be vitally important as immediate objectives—but through a change in the relationship of the system to those who live subject to its control. This means that workers and their unions need to join parents, foster parents, and youth in struggle. Reform of the system is of course an important step toward struggle for more fundamental change. In formulating demands for reform, however, we should think about whether it is consistent with changing the relationship with families. If we demand more support for families through preventive measures such as childcare, in-home assistance, and greater access to mental health and addiction treatment, for example, we should also demand that these supports be available without a finding that the parent has neglected the child as a condition of receiving the service. We also need to join our demands for support for families with wider demands for housing, higher wages, and childcare outside the traditional child welfare system. Reform demands are essential, but they should never be demands for more money for professionals to make decisions on behalf of families.

The child welfare system has also operated to reinforce oppression, first against immigrants among the growing urbanized population and Native Americans. As the earlier systems of regulating and controlling African American children—slavery and sharecropping—were abandoned, more and more African American

children entered foster care and became disproportionately represented in comparison to their share of the general population of
children. In its operation, child welfare scapegoats and subjugates
working-class women, and the law devalues family attachments for
children and parents involved with the system in ways that would
not be tolerated if applied to areas of family law not focused on the
poor. Because gender norms and standards of sexual behavior are
reinforced within families, oppression of gays, lesbians, and transgender youth also frequently plays out within families. This means
that the child welfare system becomes responsible for young people
who come into conflict with their families because they don't conform to expectations about gender identity or sexual orientation.
The system forms part of the response to this kind of oppression,
and while the overwhelming majority of those working within the
system seek to support gay, lesbian, and transgender youth, some
institutions and legislation retain oppression and discrimination.

How Capital Benefits from the Child Welfare System

While the child welfare system is seen as existing for the benefit
of children and families, the following chapters will argue that the
means chosen to organize and run the system reveal that the primary beneficiary is capital. The ends of social stability and control
take precedence over the protection and welfare of children and
families. That prioritization is systemic and does not reflect the subjective judgment or wishes of people employed within the system.
Professionals operate within the constraints of the system and are
immersed in its ideology. It is difficult for professionals to recognize
that their subjective intentions may differ radically from the function of the system as whole.

Since its inception, the foster care system has been administered
by a government and charitable establishment that reinforces the
expectations of the economic elite. Parents, foster youth, and foster
families are dominated by agencies headed by highly compensated
managers, with layers of working-class and middle-class professionals making decisions about them and the communities in which they

live. And while the individuals working on the line processing cases within the system are typically capable of recognizing the injustice embedded in the system and the larger societal oppressions that provide the context in which it operates, recognizing injustice and oppression does not bring the power to challenge it on the job. Challenging oppression requires allying with parents and communities in efforts to effect short-term reforms and long-term restructuring.

The Italian Marxist Antonio Gramsci used the term "coercive state" to describe institutions that can exercise direct power over individuals or groups, or use the threat of their power to control behavior. The child welfare system is part of the coercive state in that it has the power, frequently exercised in poor and working-class communities and rarely in more affluent communities, to seize control of a family and physically separate parent and child. In addition, however, it has tentacles reaching far into what Gramsci called "civil society," which is the network of charitable institutions, schools, churches, community-based organizations, the media, and other institutions that exercise ideology-shaping power. Ideas about what families should look like, what responsibilities parents have, and what responsibility society has for difficulties experienced by children, as well as who deserves support and who bears watching are very important in shaping the environment in which the child welfare system operates. While it is by no means unique in this—other institutions of the coercive state, including the police and military, also reach into civil society—in child welfare the coercive and ideological functions are more tangled. This is because civil institutions often help promote the dominant ideology about families and children and also participate in the exercise of coercive power by monitoring children and families, and initiating intervention.

How Should We Think About Reform?

The most overused expression in the child welfare system is "breaking the cycle." Each new reform is seen as the key to breaking the cycle of intergenerational involvement in the system. The suggestion is that the explanation for family entanglement in the system is located within individuals and family dynamics. Any professional working within the system will encounter cases of abuse that lead one to question the humanity of the parent, and it's easy to focus on individual pathology as being responsible for the suffering of children, both as victims and as potential replicators of the harm they have suffered. I maintain that the biggest long-term threat to children is capitalism, because it is ultimately responsible for the immediate dangers that warrant intervention. Policing parents and intervening in families addresses threats to individual children. By intervening based on "risk factors," however, the system inevitably casts a wide net, needlessly disrupting and traumatizing some children because they are homeless and impoverished. The measures used by the child welfare system, no matter how well intentioned or grounded in research, cannot break the cycle so long as a third or more of children in communities policed by the child welfare system are growing up in poverty.

My argument is that while the cycle cannot be broken under capitalism, the system can and must be reformed to change the relationship of the system to children and families. Reform should point the way forward to a future in which material assistance and other supports and services are provided by communities (including professionals) rallying to help families solve their problems without the need for a coercive apparatus. Struggle for reform should also be joined to broader struggles to meet the needs of children and families, and ultimately, against capitalism.

Organization of the Book

The themes to be developed by the following chapters are summarized below. These chapters will be punctuated at various points by first-person narratives by parents, youth, and professionals living or working within the system. The purpose of these narratives is to enrich the reader's understanding of the experiences of people who interact with the system in a way that the author has not—as a child who is both dependent on the system and on whom the system is dependent for its continued existence, as a parent over whom the system exerts life-changing power, or as a professional with the power to initiate, prolong, or terminate a family's involvement with the system. None of the authors whose words are included have any responsibility for the historical or political analysis in the chapters summarized below, or for any shortcomings therein.

Chapter 1 will briefly summarize the origins of the modern foster care system in the pioneering efforts of the Children's Aid Society in New York beginning in the mid-nineteenth century. The chapter will describe in detail the Children's Exodus during the Lawrence textile strike of 1912 to show the extreme response to an attempt by the working class to assert control over the protection and well-being of its children. This episode showed that the interest of the government and bourgeois charities was more in maintaining physical and ideological control over measures to protect children than in the welfare of the children themselves. The chapter will conclude with modern parallels to the assumptions and attitudes underlying the Children's Aid Society's "Orphan Trains."

Chapter 2 will trace the history of devaluing African American parents, to show the relevance of the destruction of families under slavery and semi-feudal sharecropping to the overrepresentation of Black children in foster care. The chapter will also summarize the data on racial disproportionality in foster care, drawing in large part on the seminal analysis of Dorothy Roberts. The chapter will discuss the racist backlash whereby disproportionality is seen as evidence that Black parents are simply more prone to child maltreatment, an argument used by those who wish to impose a "color-blind" regime designed to pump children through the system toward adoption as quickly as possible. The chapter will briefly describe the unique history of child removal and foster care with regard to indigenous children, with the genocidal intent of destroying Native languages, cultures, and societies. Recent developments in Indian child welfare policy will be addressed.

Chapter 3 will discuss the roots and history of regulating the reproduction and parenting of people with disabilities. The role of capitalism in turning impairment into disability will be examined, and the continuing relevance of the role of the nuclear family in social reproduction will be considered in relation to contemporary restrictions on parenting by people with disabilities.

Chapter 4 will discuss foster youth, particularly those who transition to adulthood within the system, and the system's largely unsuccessful efforts to prioritize ability to compete in the marketplace. The chapter will describe how foster youth are "commodified," in seeing themselves as a unit of production in an industry, and how an ideology of individual achievement to "break the cycle" undermines youth addressing injustice individually or collectively. Evidence of overmedication of foster children and off-label use of psychotropic medication will be discussed. This chapter will also briefly discuss the manner in which lesbian, gay, transgender, bisexual, and questioning (LGTBQ) youth are often ill served by the foster care system. This occurs not only in jurisdictions in which homophobia has been codified into the laws governing the system, but even in jurisdictions that try to reconcile a relatively new commitment to equality with dependence on nongovernmental organizations hostile to LGTBQ people.

Chapter 5 will discusses the role of unpaid foster parents and their status within the public and private bureaucracy.

Chapter 6 will deal with the related but distinct juvenile justice system. The chapter will discuss its relationship to child welfare in terms of the number of "crossover youth" who are successively or simultaneously governed by both systems.

Chapter 7 will discuss frontline staff within the system, with an emphasis on the professional cultures that shape interaction between parents and professionals—social work and, to a lesser extent, the legal profession. The history and potential for radical practice within the field will be surveyed. The chapter will describe the pressures on child welfare workers that contribute to aggressiveness and dehumanization of parents. It will also consider the potential for social justice unionism.

Chapter 8 will discuss the questions raised by the decline in foster care placements. It will argue that part of the reason for the decline is grassroots organizing and advocacy by parents. Another is a decision to change the means used to regulate families. It will argue that the shrinkage of the foster care system does not fundamentally change the nature of the system or necessarily demonstrate its success, given the wide variation in removal rates among cities with no corresponding impact on child safety.

Chapter 9 will attempt to differentiate true fundamental reform that would democratize children's services and redefine its purposes from incremental system change led by professional organizations and existing institutions. It will also critique the emphasis on Scandinavian-style social democratic models of child welfare support. While this model offers desirable material support for families, it has also been associated with enormous discretion for professionals and strong class bias. The chapter will advocate directions for reform that are consistent with working to change the social relationships of capitalism.

Chapter 10 will expand on the Marxist concept of social reproduction, which links the production of goods and services with the reproduction of human beings to replenish the workforce. This function of social reproduction provides a basis for enforcing expectations of family structure and for regulating family life. Capitalism also depends on relegating a significant percentage of families to life in poverty. The institutions of the child welfare system are among those that regulate families—using coercive and ideological means. The system also functions as a safety valve. If the blame for the plight of poor children can be situated in family pathology rather than in racialized child poverty, the threat to the legitimacy of capitalism is reduced.

Chapter 11 will look at what Marxists say about families. Although Marxists have been caricatured as seeking to abolish or collectivize the parent-child relationship, my contention is that Marxism actually seeks a richer, more satisfying relationship for parents, children, and the communities in which they live.

* * *

This modest book is written to serve two immodest purposes. The first is to encourage people living within the system, either as subjects of its power or as functionaries, to think about radical change, both in the institutions and activities of the system and in the communities and society in which the system operates. For the author, working within the foster care system prompted a journey from vague and squishy social democratic politics to revolutionary socialism. I felt the need to connect my politics with the system I had become part of, and for my political life to be active and connected to broad struggles against racism and capitalism. It was both gratifying and humbling to realize that parent organizers I met were way ahead of me in connecting their struggles with activism against mass incarceration and police violence, for a living wage and labor rights, and against oppression wherever it occurs in the world.

The second purpose is to apply specific theoretical insights from Marxist traditions to analyze the institutions that regulate poor and working-class families, with the goal of enriching discussion of reform and linking it to a struggle for "socialism from below," which must begin with fights for democratic power over the institutions of oppression. To that end, I have tried to make the discussion of these concepts as accessible and jargon free as possible, and I hope readers interested in child welfare policy but unfamiliar with Marxism will engage critically but patiently and open-mindedly with these arguments.

ONE

The "Orphan Trains"—Then and Now

Origins

The fear of a dependent and potentially disruptive class of people outside the mainstream of economic life has long been a feature of child welfare and definitely remains so today. In pre-industrial America, there were informal practices to help needy families by providing some basic assistance at the parish or community level, along with the opportunity to place children on farms or as apprentices to provide for their care. Children were economic assets close to home, so there wasn't a need for state intervention or organized charity. As the population grew and became urbanized, and as mass immigration fueled the growth of cities, there was a growing consciousness of the urban poor among the ruling class. Early responses included jailing children for vagrancy, and warehousing them in poorhouses. Motivated in part by fear of producing a criminal underclass, a patrician reformer named Charles Loring Brace created the Children's Aid Society in New York, which became the model for modern foster care. Brace made the argument that it was more humane to place children in homes than in jail, which is hard to argue with, but the fact that he referred to the children to whom he ostensibly dedicated his life's work as "the dangerous classes" gives a not-so-subtle hint about where he was coming from. It was not solely—or even primarily—a humanitarian impulse that motivated Brace, but a fear that the elite class he represented would lose control of the growing US cities.

Brace made the argument that the US-born children of foreign-born parents were more dangerous than the unruly "proletaires" of Europe. In a peculiar formulation of an argument of American exceptionalism, he claimed that the more vibrant atmosphere of American urban life could make the children of immigrants a greater threat to order. In *The Life of the Street Rats* (1872), Brace wrote:

> The intensity of the American temperament is felt in every fibre of these children of poverty and vice. Their crimes have the unrestrained and sanguinary character of a race accustomed to overcome all obstacles. They rifle a bank, where English thieves pick a pocket; they murder, where European proletaires cudgel or fight with fists; in a riot, they begin what seems about to be the sacking of a city, where English rioters would merely batter policemen, or smash lamps.

In appealing for support from his own class, Brace reminded his readers:

> These boys and girls, it should be remembered, will soon form the great lower class of our city. They will influence elections; they may shape the policy of the city; they will assuredly, if unre-claimed, poison society all around them. They will help to form the great multitude of robbers, thieves, and vagrants who are now such a burden on the law-respecting community.[1]

Brace claimed he was saving children—mainly Catholic immigrants—from the evil influence of their parents and communities, and placing them with good American Protestant families, preferably far away from the city. He organized groups of children on what became known as "Orphan Trains" and sent them west in search of homes. (It's noteworthy that only a small percentage of the riders of the Orphan Trains were actually orphans. The popularization of the name is an indication that the existence of biological parents was an inconvenient circumstance for the bourgeois charities.)

The assumption was that handing these children off to strangers with no real vetting was better than providing assistance to their families or placing them with a relative or in their own communities. Local governments and charitable institutions maintained a distinction between the "deserving poor" (widows, orphans, workers who became disabled) and the "undeserving poor" (unmarried mothers, the unemployed). The deserving poor were victims of circumstance and deserved assistance, while the undeserving poor just lacked the moral fiber to help themselves, so any assistance they were given had to be regulated and coupled with moral reeducation. They had to be stigmatized to prevent others from becoming dependent. Foster care for children with living parents was mostly associated with the undeserving poor. In time, Catholic organizations formed to place Catholic children, and Jewish organizations to place Jewish children, but they were modeled on Children's Aid without the bias toward Protestantism.

The Children's Exodus

The two-month strike of textile workers in Lawrence, Massachusetts that began in January 1912, later to be known as the "Bread and Roses Strike," was a milestone in US labor history. One of the most remarkable aspects of the textile strike was the manner in which the strikers and their allies organized to care for the children of the striking workers. As the strike wore on, the Italian Socialist Federation presented a plan inspired by strikes in Italy but never before used in a US strike. This became known as the "Children's Exodus," and it can fairly be characterized as a working-class form of foster care.[2]

Allies in the labor movement recruited and screened strike-supporting families, and parents and children in Lawrence were prepared for the pain of separation. Two groups totaling more than 250 children left Lawrence. Money was contributed by strike supporters for the care, support, and entertainment of the children. All were seen by doctors, and most made their first trips to zoos, circuses, and museums.

The support of the working class for the exodus was countered by howls of outrage from the government authorities and charitable establishment in Lawrence and beyond. Although no laws had been broken, after the first exodus, the commander of the militia troops guarding the textile mills announced that no further groups of children would be permitted to leave the city. The head of the Massachusetts Society for the Prevention of Cruelty to Children lamented that he had no legal authority to prevent the removals. Mayor Michael Scanlon pronounced that it was the city's responsibility to take care of children if their parents were unable to do so. Showing a stunning lack of appreciation for irony, the mayor of a city in which the use of legal and illegal child labor was ubiquitous accused the strikers of "exploiting" the children. Newspapers trumpeted the fact that the children had been sent to stay with anarchists and socialists, who would be a corrupting influence on innocent children.

An attempt to send a third contingent was blocked by police, who clubbed parents into submission, arresting some with their children. The judge fined the parents for disturbing the peace, and then sent the "neglected" children to the local poorhouse to be cared for by the city. While the standards of care were demonstrably lower in the institution than in the homes of the volunteer host families, the children could no doubt be kept safe from radical contamination.

The Children's Exodus is important not simply as part of the history of the strike but for what it says about bourgeois assumptions about child welfare intervention. The oppressive response illustrates the point that the child welfare system—which was still emerging in its modern form in 1912—exists in large part to exercise social control over poor families, and to meet the needs of capital before those of families. By demonstrating its own capacity to organize an alternative based on working-class solidarity and respect for parents, the organizers of the exodus had issued a challenge the system was unable to ignore.

The Orphan Train Mentality Today

The arrogance of the system toward poor and working-class parents is still with us, and the Orphan Train mentality is echoed in the treatment of the children of undocumented parents today. A yearlong investigation by the Applied Research Center, the publisher of *Colorlines*, found that more than five thousand children of undocumented parents were remanded into foster care when their parents were detained for deportation.[3] In one case, a mother learned at the airport that her child would not be accompanying her to Guatemala, and a judge later reasoned that it was undoubtedly in the child's best interest to be raised by a middle-class family in the United States rather than return to an impoverished village in Guatemala with a parent who had committed the "crime" of crossing the border illegally.

Similarly, a 2011 investigation by National Public Radio found that South Dakota routinely ignores federal law in order to remove Native American children for placement with middle-class white families.[4] This builds on a long, genocidal history of removal and placement in Indian boarding schools, on the assumption that it was necessary to separate children from their families and communities in order to integrate them into (white) "civilization."

The condescending attitude that the essential problem with poor families is some kind of values deficit is usually associated with political and social conservatives, but is also typical of centrist and progressive Democrats. In 1994, shortly before the Republican landslide that made him speaker of the House of Representatives, Newt Gingrich suggested slashing welfare and putting the children made destitute as a result in orphanages. In response to the ensuing backlash, Gingrich cited the 1938 movie *Boys Town* as supporting data for his contention that institutional care could be transformative and morally uplifting.[5]

Gingrich was widely ridiculed, but the idea enjoyed support from others on the right who framed it in a more serious way. The Heritage Foundation promoted institutional care, as did conservative heavyweights William Bennett and Charles Murray. Murray, fresh off his attempt to revive pseudo-scientific eugenics with his argument in *The Bell Curve* that Blacks were less intelligent than whites, argued for massive adoption of "illegitimate" children and institutional care for some who couldn't be adopted. Murray offered reassurance to those who found the word "orphanage" unpalatable, suggesting they could "think of them as twenty-four-hour-a-day preschools." He also suggested that "those who prattle about the importance of keeping children with their biological mothers may wish to spend some time in a patrol car or with a social worker seeing what the reality of life with welfare-dependent biological mothers can be like."[6]

Republican representative Jim Talent introduced a bill to cut income and housing assistance to unmarried mothers and divert the money the federal government would save to states to create "group homes" for the mothers and children where the mothers could be closely monitored and taught how to raise their children properly.[7] The Right never really pushed the idea of orphanages, possibly because they are far more expensive than the savings from cutting children off welfare, but the discussion of these proposals was part of an aggressive campaign—not at all subtle in its racism and misogyny—to blame persistent poverty on "welfare mothers" corrupted by a liberal entitlement culture.

The Democratic Party had long embraced the "personal responsibility" argument, most famously in Bill Clinton's 1992 campaign pledge to "end welfare as we know it." This endeavor eventually resulted in his signing the Personal Responsibility and Work Opportunity Reconciliation Act (PRWORA) as he campaigned for reelection four years later. PRWORA was Clinton's signature accomplishment in welfare "reform." According to an admiring biographer, Clinton had discovered the "answer to the 'culture of poverty' arguments long posed by conservatives—but it was an answer that combined conservative values ('responsibility') with liberal spending ('opportunity')," which was "perhaps, the purest demonstration of the substance and possibilities of the Third Way."[8]

Even more liberal Democrats who protested the harshness of many of the provisions of PRWORA accepted the basic premise that it was the limitations of individuals that kept them in poverty. Peter Edelman, who resigned his position as a Clinton appointee to the US Department of Health and Human Services to protest PRWORA, made the argument that welfare recipients wouldn't be able to hold jobs even with work incentives: "The labor market, even in its current relatively heated state, is not friendly to people with little education and few marketable skills, poor work habits, and various personal and family problems that interfere with regular and punctual attendance."[9]

So while Democrats didn't propose a return to old-school orphanages, they certainly engaged in victim blaming when it came to the parents of children in poverty. In the area of child welfare policy, Clinton's signature accomplishment was the Adoption and Safe Families Act (ASFA) of 1997. ASFA provided a new emphasis on a fast track to adoption by providing financial incentives and eliminating barriers to termination of parental rights. Proponents of ASFA said it was "child-centered," in contrast to previous "parent-centered legislation."

As law professor and author Dorothy Roberts pointed out, the discussion of ASFA was framed around the assumption that parents' and children's rights are in opposition to one another.[10] Such an assumption would never be made about white families thought to be closer to the American middle-class ideal,[11] but poor families, particularly poor Black families, are valued far less and accorded far less deference.

A KNOCK ON THE DOOR*

My Family Needed Support, Not Separation

By Philneia Timmons

About 7 p.m. there was a knock on the door. I was afraid I already knew who it was and that my family was in trouble.

The problems started when my son was ten years old and his grandfather died. His grandfather was more like a father to him than his own father. Many times when my son would visit their house, his father wouldn't be there, but his grandfather was, and they'd sit and talk and have fun.

Anger in His Eyes

Before his grandfather died, my son was basically well behaved. After, he had so many questions, like, "Where do people go when they die?" I could see the anger in his eyes and hear the fear in his voice. I believe his feelings were even stronger because losing his grandfather brought up the sad feelings he had about his father not being around.

My son began to retaliate against his father, me, and just life itself. He was getting in trouble just about every day in school. He wasn't working and he was being disruptive. I was running to the school so often that I had to quit my job. I felt so frustrated, I didn't know what to do.

Eventually I started to hit him, even though I don't believe in hitting kids. One night I hit him with a belt because his teacher had called to say he had cursed in class. He screamed so loud when I hit him that I stopped, but the damage was already done. The next day the school informed me that they had found bruises on my son's body. ACS came that night.

"We Received a Call"

When I answered the door, there was a social worker there named Mrs. R., her assistant, and a police officer. They said they wanted to ask me a few questions.

---

* Reprinted with permission from *Rise*, a magazine written by parents affected by the child welfare system: www.risemagazine.org. This story appeared in the Spring 2006 issue of *Rise*.

Mrs. R. handed me a paper and asked to see my children. (I also have a daughter.) She said, "We received a call from your school that your son had bruises on his arm and upper thigh." Mrs. R. insisted that I lift my children's clothing. When I did not comply, Mrs. R. asked her assistant to lift them and then she took pictures of the bruises on my son's left arm and thigh. Then she told me my children were being removed.

As they left my house, I felt like a piece of my heart was being ripped out.

"My Children Need Me"

After my children were taken, I went through terrible pressure and depression, not knowing whether my children were safe. I could not eat or sleep many days and nights.

I felt so much anger. I'd often ask myself why ACS couldn't help while my children were home. "My children need and want to be with me," I'd think. "If you're helping us, then help us together. I'll do whatever it takes, you can still make your home visits, every day if you'd like. Just please release my children to me."

Emotions Running Wild

Then there was the anger that I felt toward myself. Growing up, my mother would often hit me with belts and even extension cords. Sometimes her anger was out of control. I felt mistreated and misunderstood, and I would rarely speak to my mother even though what I was looking for was guidance, acceptance, attention, and a way out from the madness and the pressures that I felt as a child.

When I gave birth to my son, I vowed that I would never hit my children the way my mother hit me. But when my son's behavior got so bad, I was angry and desperate and I just wanted to do something to stop it. I knew how I acted after my mom hit me—I was so hurt and afraid of another beating that I'd stop doing whatever it was I just got hit for. I thought a beating would make my son stop, too.

I never imagined it would mean I would lose my kids. I was so angry at myself because my children had to suffer for what I'd done. I cried myself to sleep many nights. My emotions were really running wild because I loved my kids so much and it hurt so much to lose them.

Starting to Cooperate

For the first couple of months, my anger kept me from doing what the system told me I needed to do. I wasn't going to counseling because I felt I didn't need it. Whenever I went to see the caseworker, I wasn't cooperative because I just wanted to smack her.

But after a few months of rebelling, I realized that I couldn't let that continue because there was too much at stake—my children. The longer it took me to get proper visits with them, the harder it was going to be to get them back permanently.

So I prayed, I read the Bible, I told myself again and again to calm down. I forced myself to get my emotions under control. I also decided that if I was going to change my situation, I couldn't just depend on my caseworker or my lawyer. I would have to learn what I could about the system myself.

I Was in Control

I went to the library and the librarian gave me *The Family and Medical Leave Act*, a very thick blue book with information about the system. It said I had the right to visit my children, the right to be a part of making decisions about their medical care and education. It said I could even attend parent-teacher conferences.

I wrote the information down in a notebook. With that knowledge, I would go to meetings at the agency or ACS and I would quote different sections of the book. I wanted them to think I had real power behind me, so when they asked me where I got my information from, I'd lie and say that I had my own lawyer. I spoke calmly but firmly and I carried myself in a way that let them know I was in control.

Many times I had to hold back tears, anger, frustration that felt like a ball of fire. Inside I often felt hot and furious. But I thought about ice, snow, and winter to calm me down. I controlled my temper, and it paid off.

A Person, Not a Case

The agency began to look at me as a person, not as a caseload and docket number. It helped, too, that I began to comply more fully with their requirements. I went to therapy and I completed two parenting skills classes. I also began working at the Child Welfare Organizing Project, where parents who have children in the system advocate to improve how the system treats parents.

Because of all that, I gained permission to take my children to school every day. I took them to doctors' appointments and therapy, too. Eventually I was allowed to spend time with them on the weekends.

Accepting My Son's Ways

Soon I realized that I had to calm down, not only with the system but with my son, too. For a while after my son went into care, he had even more problems than he'd had before. His behavior in school grew worse and he didn't want to do any work at all. He was probably sad and mad that he'd been taken from me.

I was frustrated but I told myself that all I could do was talk to him. I just told him over and over how important school is and that I'd gone to school too. Maybe because I was calmer, he began to respond a little better to me. I also think his therapist helped him. Sometimes I felt uncomfortable with her—I felt like she was judging me—but my son liked her.

One day my son said to me, "Mommy, you're always telling me what to do." He said, "Ma, I would feel better if you said, 'Just try to do it.'" When he said that I realized that maybe I was too demanding and I had to accept that my son had ways of his own.

Help Us at Home

Still, there were limits to how much I could do until I finally was given a caseworker who really worked with me. I've had three caseworkers during the two years my children have been in care. The first two never once made a home visit.

A few months ago, I was given my third caseworker and she's beautiful. I almost love her. She saw how hard I was trying, and she gave me weekend and overnight visits. I appreciate that she acts like she trusts me and cares about my children and me.

Soon my two children will be released into my care full time. I have some worries how long it will take my children to get used to being home. Sometimes my son and I still have our turbulences. But he and I have grown and our relationship has improved.

Looking back, I did need help with my son because I felt out of control and that was affecting my relationship with him. But I don't believe that my children needed to be taken from me. I wish that I had been given help while my children were still with me instead of having them thrown into the system.

Philneia's children are now home and she worked at the time of the writing as a parent advocate with ACS.

TWO

Moving Toward a Racialized Child Welfare System

Regulating Black Children Under Slavery and Jim Crow

One area of dramatic change in foster care is in the treatment of African American children. Early on, there were a few segregated orphanages, but the foster care system largely excluded Black children, for better or worse, because they primarily lived in the rural South, where there was very little state intervention or organized charity. Instead, first there was slavery, where the legal head of the family was the slavemaster, not the parent of a child born into slavery.

The destruction of families was one of the most vicious effects of chattel slavery, and provided a powerful impetus for Black resistance. It's important to note how often heroic figures in the stories of Black resistance to slavery had experienced horrendous disruption of family relationships.

Denmark Vesey, who planned a slave rebellion in South Carolina in 1822, was a formerly enslaved Black man who was unable to earn enough to purchase the freedom of his wife and children, and Nat Turner, who led a rebellion in Virginia in 1831, was also separated from his wife and children because they were the legal property of a different man than the one purported to own Turner. Sojourner Truth was enslaved in New York during the period slavery was gradually abolished in the state. When she learned that one of her sons had been illegally sold and taken to Alabama to avoid his being freed, she took the extraordinary step of swearing out a criminal complaint against his former master and forcing him to retrieve her son to avoid arrest.[1] Harriet Tubman's family was torn apart when three of her sisters were sold, and her mother hid one of her brothers to prevent his being sold. When the boy was finally located, Harriet's mother actually prevented the sale by threatening to kill her master if he tried to take the child away. Later, Harriet herself began her career as a conductor on the Underground Railroad when, after escaping slavery in Maryland, she returned to free her niece, who was about to be separated from her family by sale.[2]

One of the participants in the raid on Harpers Ferry, Virginia, in 1859 was a formerly enslaved man named Dangerfield Newby, whose Virginia slavemaster had provided for his emancipation in his will. Newby's wife, Harriet, was the legal property of a neighbor, meaning that at birth, each of their seven children also became the property of Harriet's master. Since Virginia law provided that upon emancipation an enslaved person had to leave the state, Newby's newfound freedom also meant his separation from his wife and his seven children. He went to Pennsylvania to work for hire and save money to purchase the freedom of his family, a nearly impossible task. Newby and Harriet exchanged anguished letters, and Harriet shared her fear that her owner's precarious finances would result in his selling off one or more member of the family. Under the circumstances, his own emancipation meant little to Newby, who signed on to the Harpers Ferry insurrection in the hopes of sparking a wider rebellion in Virginia. The white and Black participants intended to establish a provisional republic, holding mountain territory in what became West Virginia, in the belief that this would force the hand of the northern states to overthrow the slave regime. An article in the provisional constitution drafted before the raid read: "The marriage relation shall be at all times respected, and families kept together as far as possible, and broken families encouraged to unite, and intelligence offices established for that purpose."[3]

After Emancipation, one of the first tasks of the Freedmen's Bureau established by the federal government as a Reconstruction measure was to facilitate the reunification of families separated by slavery. Two trends quickly emerged, however. As white opposition to measures to make radical changes to the power structure of the South limited the possibilities for real reform, the Freedmen's Bureau increasingly became a "vast labor bureau"—an intermediary for Black fathers, as heads of reunited families, to enter into contracts with white landowners to supply the families' labor.[4] Pressure was also put on families to "apprentice" their children to plantation owners, as a means of preserving the plantation system deemed essential to the economy of the South. The Black Codes allowed Black children to be declared vagrants and placed as apprentices, making their labor available to plantation owners. Mississippi went so far as to give the child's former slave master priority in acquiring his labor, effectively reestablishing the master and slave relationship.[5]

There was, in any event, no attempt to re-create or strengthen family life for the child. For a time, white northern reformers became captivated by an idealized mission of civilizing "Freedom's Children," the offspring of former slaves. The assumption was that their parents were incapable of contributing to this effort, so the roles of newly established schools was in part to counter the influence of the ignorant and debased adult Black population. In an echo of the Orphan Train concept, some Black children were sent north to live with—and work for—white families, and "the irony of sending former slave children hundreds of miles away to fill the needs of northern employers for dishwashers and household servants—in the aftermath of a system of slavery that had divided black families for generations and a sectional conflict that had ended the interstate trade in human beings—seems to have escaped some of their sponsors entirely."[6] In any event, the importance of Black children to the economy of the South resulted in active discouragement of this trend.

After Reconstruction, repression and economic pressure ensured that Black children remained a source of cheap labor. While some Black children entered foster care, usually in the North and usually in inferior living conditions, most Black children remained in the South, where they were regarded as a source of labor rather than a population in need of care.

THE COLOR OF HOPE*

Race Can Affect Whether Parents Get the Support to Overcome

By Shrounda Selivanoff and Alise Hegle

My child welfare story (Shrounda) began when I moved into a neighborhood high in drug use and poverty. I was an African American woman in my mid-thirties, married with two children. I was arrogant—I thought I could control my drug use and that my surroundings wouldn't affect me. Instead I found myself in the depth of an ever-evolving addiction. I went from using alcohol and cocaine to using crack daily. I desired so much out of life, but my drug use eroded my motivation and my commitment to succeed.

My addiction lasted for eight years. During that time, my husband and I divorced; my younger son went to live with his father while my older son moved in with a friend's family. Then, in 2007, when I gave birth to my third child, child protective services were immediately called in and they took my daughter from me.

At first I did not feel the despair. Drugs and alcohol numbed me to the life-changing event. My addiction also led me to cut myself off from whatever services the system offered. For a year, I missed appointments and had only sporadic interactions with the department, the foster family, and my daughter.

Undeserving in Their Eyes

But I also believe the system was not sincere in wanting to help me. In a meeting I attended to decide my daughter's future, her foster mother asked: "How could you return the child to someone like her?" I found out later that the social worker told the foster family that I had little hope of reunification with my daughter.

I felt those judgments, and they incubated into self-doubt and self-loathing. I felt like a statistic moving through the system rather than a person making human connections. The report on paper outlined a deplorable

---

* Reprinted with permission from *Rise*, a magazine written by parents affected by the child welfare system: *www.risemagazine.org*. This story appeared in the Fall 2014 issue of *Rise*.

woman. In truth, neither the system nor I knew who I really was or who I might turn out to be.

Luckily, I did have the support of my family and lawyer. Eventually, I also found support from remarkable counselors, employers, and friends. Each one, in my darkest hour, held the candle, allowing me to see a different picture of me and a different possibility for my life.

After a year of noncompliance, it took me another year and four months to reunify with my daughter. But even after I'd made so many changes, my daughter's foster family was still appalled. While I truly believe they loved my daughter, I think the stereotype they saw in me made it hard for them to see me as anything other than undeserving.

"Unlikely to Ever Change"

I (Alise) first became involved with the child welfare system as a twenty-five-year-old White woman. I spent most of my life in darkness and utter chaos; an existence comprised of poor choices, low self-worth, and inadequate coping mechanisms, including drug use. When I gave birth to my daughter, she was immediately placed in foster care, partly due to the seven-year prison sentence I was facing for committing property crimes to fuel my addiction.

I was blessed with the opportunity to go to treatment instead of prison through Drug Offenders Sentencing Alternatives, a statewide program for people charged with drug crimes. It is an opportunity many judges might not have offered me, given the multiple property-related felonies I'd been convicted of. But my judge decided I would never have committed those crimes if it weren't for my addiction.

Still, during the first eleven months, I received no visits with my daughter. My caseworker said in court that it was unlikely I was ever going to change and the best outcome would be to allow my daughter to be adopted. When I heard that, I was terrified—and my belief that I was worthless penetrated to the core of my being.

Fortunately, I, too, had support—from my mother, my attorney, and the social worker in my attorney's office. It was their uplifting messages that allowed me to believe I could be the parent and advocate I've become. Once I began having visits with my daughter, I was able to reunify with her in just four months.

The Color of Hope

For both of us, Shrounda and Alise, Black and White, it was the power of people inside and outside the system who truly believed in us that allowed us to see ourselves as more than drug-addicted bad mothers and overcome. We are now both employed as parent advocates in Washington State, at the advocacy organization Catalyst for Kids (Alise) and Evergreen Manor Inpatient Treatment (Shrounda). We also volunteer on many committees aimed at making the child welfare system a more supportive place for families. What the research suggests, however, and what we've seen, is that race plays a role in whether parents and children find the support that allows them to succeed.

The differences start before parents come to the attention of the child welfare system. In poor neighborhoods of color, most parents see child protective services as the people who come to take your kids and nothing else. Many parents are too afraid of losing their kids to ask for help.

Once parents are in the system, their lives are in the hands of caseworkers who are over-burdened and under-supported. Research has found that parents of color receive fewer contacts by their caseworkers, and fewer and lower quality mental health and drug treatment services as well.

The Color of Trust

Race can also make it harder for parents of color to trust the system.

When I (Shrounda) would visit my daughter in my agency's visiting room, seeing so many Black families like mine added to the shame I already felt. Visits are supposed to be an opportunity to bond with your child. But visiting rooms are often such depressing places they almost seem designed to add to parents' self-loathing. When I visited my daughter, I felt segregated, discriminated against, and inadequate.

Recently, I (Alise) was mentoring an African American parent who said, "My social worker can't stand me because I'm Black." The parent had witnessed the social worker being nice to a White family, but consistently dismissive to her. Neither the parent nor I knew whether the difference in attitude was because of race. But the parent's perception of racism added to the tension that existed between them.

All these differences add up to grave consequences, according to statistics compiled by Casey Family Programs. In 2012, a Black child was nearly twice as likely to enter foster care as a White child, while a Native American child was almost two and half times more likely to enter care. Once Black and Native American children are in care, they stay there longer and experience more placements. They also go home or get adopted less often.

In 2012, Black children made up 22 percent of children entering foster care but 35 percent of children who aged out of the system. While 8 percent of White children who entered foster care before the age of three aged out without ever finding a permanent home, 14 percent of Native American children and 17 percent of Black children did. That means that one in every six Black babies that enters foster care spends almost her or his entire childhood there.

When I (Alise) was navigating the system, I never thought that my skin color might contribute to the success I eventually had. I still believe that a higher power moved mountains to allow me to reunify with my daughter. But today I also know that, statistically speaking, the fact that I'm White made it more likely that I would get the breaks I needed.

Documenting Disproportionality

In the last ten years, some systems have started tracking the numbers of children of color in foster care and making changes.

In 2002, in our home state of Washington, Black social workers in King County (which includes Seattle) worked on their own time to gather data to demonstrate that children of color went into care in higher numbers and stayed in care longer as well.

In 2004, the King County Coalition on Racial Disproportionality published the first data showing that a Black child in King Country was three times more likely to be in foster care than a White child, while a Native American child was approximately eight times more likely to be in care.

Then, in 2007, the Washington State Legislature established the Washington State Racial Disproportionality Advisory Committee. I (Shrounda) am a member of this committee.

Working for Change

One of the first steps the committee took was to develop a tool that asks agencies to consider the impact [their] policies might have on people of color and includes such questions as: "Were there representatives of different racial groups at the table in development of this policy?" Washington State's Children's Administration has recently begun to use this tool to analyze its policies.

One change it has made as a result is in the criminal background check relatives have to pass in order to care for their kin. The administration realized these background checks prevented many children of color from being raised by family, even though past convictions were sometimes decades old. Ultimately, our state legislature significantly reduced the list of crimes that barred people from ever having a child placed in their care.

We hope this essential work continues—here in Washington State and across the country. When I (Shrounda) look at our policy makers, I often feel that the problems of my community are an eyesore they'd rather not see. But I also know that with effort, it is possible to decrease the number of children of color in foster care.

As a parent advocate, I (Alise) know how powerless and hopeless many families feel because their children are placed with strangers. When you add to this the pain of discrimination, both real and perceived, those feelings can become almost unbearable. The child welfare system should empower people who are already disempowered, not disempower them further. My daughter is at home with her mommy. It pains me to think that might have been less likely to happen if I weren't White.

Black Children and Foster Care

The transformation of foster care into a system predominantly populated by Black children occurred over the decades following the mechanization of southern agriculture and the urbanization of the Black poor, following the massive shifts in the Black population from the rural South to northern cities between 1910 and 1970. The federal Aid to Families with Dependent Children (AFDC) program, which began as a Depression-era entitlement from which Blacks were often excluded by discriminatory state eligibility standards, began to grow during the 1950s and 1960s.

It was never a program that primarily benefited Blacks, but as the exclusionary barriers were struck down and a higher percentage of Blacks left the semi-slavery of sharecropping for segregated urban neighborhoods with little access to stable employment, more Black families ended up on AFDC.

When Malcolm X was six and living with his family in Michigan, his father was killed, likely by white supremacists. In his autobiography, Malcolm describes how the desperate poverty of the family led to the intrusion of the "Welfare people" and the deterioration of the family:

> When the state Welfare people began coming to our house, we would come from school sometimes and find them talking with our mother, asking a thousand questions. They acted and looked at her, and at us, and around in our house, in a way that had about it the feeling—at least for me—that we were not people. . . . But the monthly Welfare check was their pass. . . . We all heard them call my mother "crazy" to her face for refusing good meat. It meant nothing to them even when she explained that we had never eaten pork, that it was against her religion as a Seventh Day Adventist. . . They told us, "She's crazy for refusing food.". . . . Eventually my mother suffered a complete breakdown, and the court orders were finally signed. They took her to the State Mental Hospital at Kalamazoo. . . A Judge McClellan in Lansing had authority over me and all of my brothers and sisters. We were "state children," court wards; he had the full say-so over us. A white man in charge of a black man's children! Nothing but legal, modern slavery—however kindly intentioned.[7]

While Malcolm X's experience in prison is often cited as an influence on his later political consciousness, his experience in state care is less frequently discussed. In his excellent and controversial 2011 biography of Malcolm X, Manning Marable notes that the sequence of events may differ in some respects from Malcolm's account, but he doesn't try to assess the impact this involvement with the child welfare system had on Malcolm's political development.[8]

Malcolm X's characterization of the actions of the system's "home-wreckers" as "legal, modern slavery—however kindly intentioned" reflects sentiments that are common in Black neigh-borhoods where child welfare investigations are most concentrated. That assessment of institutional racism in the system has also res-onated with the some of the most radical critics within the child welfare system.

The National Association of Black Social Workers (NABSW) has been one such source of criticism, especially on the issue of "transracial adoption," which typically means white couples adopt-ing Black babies and infants. In 1972, the NABSW issued a position paper opposing transracial adoption, which it publicly condemned as a form of genocide. NABSW also made the case that advocates of a color-blind approach to transracial adoption disregarded the harm to children from loss of identity and community, and from lack of preparation to encounter racism outside their home environment.[9]

NABSW had some success in advocating for matching chil-dren with foster/adoptive parents by race, sometimes by policy, and sometimes by unwritten practice.[10] A backlash emerged to the NABSW position, led by those who argued for eliminating barriers to speedy adoptions. The most powerful voice of the backlash came to be Elizabeth Bartholet of Harvard Law School, who described unadopted Black foster children in the title of her influential 1999 book *Nobody's Children*.[11] As we will see, Bartholet's arguments amount to a denial that institutional racism exists in child welfare, and an assertion that Black parents are simply more prone to mis-treat their children. She has also said that disproportionate adop-tion of Black children by white adoptive parents should not be a concern because they tend to have the financial resources to adopt more children.

Race-conscious placement was blamed for "foster care drift," with a growing population of children remaining in care awaiting adoptive homes. The real problem, however, was the surge in foster care placements and termination of parental rights as a consequence of the war on drugs. By 1995, half of all indicated cases of child maltreatment involved a caregiver alleged to be chemically depen-dent. Factors contributing to lengthy stays in foster care and loss of parental rights included draconian sentencing laws that shattered families, long waits for often ineffective treatment programs, treatment programs that separated parents and children for long periods of time, and lack of jobs and affordable housing for parents with drug convictions.[12] Nevertheless, pro-adoption lobbyists targeted racial matching as the cause of children remaining in foster care for long periods.

In 1993, Congress passed the Multi-Ethnic Placement Act (MEPA), introduced by liberal Democratic senators Howard Metzenbaum and Carol Moseley Braun, which limits the ability of foster care agencies to consider race or ethnicity as a factor in selecting foster or adoptive homes. The law didn't prohibit all use of race and culture as a factor, but it did prohibit any consideration that would delay adoption. Two years later MEPA was amended to prohibit use of race as a factor altogether. Bartholet favored more aggressive enforcement but hailed the law as amended in 1996 in expansive terms, saying "same race matching policies were direct descendants of white supremacy and black separatism. And I think that is not the path our country has chosen to take for very good reasons. And I see MEPA as directly in line with the interracial marriage case *Loving v. Virginia.*"[13]

Bartholet has also become the go-to expert on international adoption, arguing after the 2010 Haitian earthquake that adoptions of Haitian children should be expedited, because "social science makes clear that international adoptees are extremely well treated, with their prospects for overcoming early deprivation dramatically improved by early placement."[14]

Whether she is discussing victims of the Haitian earthquake or the American economy, Bartholet's prescription for "unparented children" is the same. What matters is the speed with which we can funnel them into new, better homes with new, better, wealthier parents.

While I find the NABSW position too absolute, I find the rhetoric of adoption advocates even more troubling. It is often steeped in "culture of poverty" arguments that devalue any connection to relatives and the community where a child has lived. So while I don't favor an absolute ban on transracial adoption in all cases, neither do I favor MEPA's ban on consideration of race as a factor in the name of "color-blindness." At a minimum, if prospective parents don't recognize that they will be raising a child in a society in which racism will be a real and continuous threat, or if they somehow think they are rescuing the child from a pathological culture of poverty, how can they be appropriate parents?

In my somewhat limited experience in New York, I found that MEPA was widely ignored in practice, and there was limited awareness about its provisions. In selecting pre-adoptive foster homes, workers had practical concerns that ranged from whether parents knew how to care for the child's hair to whether the child would be isolated from the culture of the family he or she had been born into.

Prior to 1962, foster care was solely funded by states. AFDC was federally funded, but states determined eligibility. Louisiana and other states excluded homes where children were born out of wedlock, because they said the parents were presumptively "unfit," and the policy was not to give money to unfit parents. Louisiana tried to cut twenty-three thousand children from the rolls in one fell swoop. Arthur Flemming, President Kennedy's secretary of health, education, and welfare, ruled that states could only exclude those children from the AFDC rolls if they investigated the homes and found the parents unfit, in which case they'd have to remove the children. There was an outcry from states fearing escalating foster care costs if they targeted unmarried parents for investigation instead of just summarily cutting their children from the AFDC rolls. In a remarkable demonstration of what happens when liberals and conservatives work together in the field of child welfare, Congress responded by codifying the "Flemming Rule" in federal law, and allowing AFDC funds to be used to offset the extra costs of foster care.[15]

AFDC became more unpopular as the scapegoating of "welfare queens" became a vicious meme reinforcing racist and sexist stereotypes and fueling the impulse to police poor families. The next phase in the story relates to the liberal response to the racist backlash against the civil rights movement, the war on poverty, and the welfare rights movement. Liberals in Congress decided to decouple the issues of poverty and racism from child welfare, and to ride the crest of a wave of national concern over child abuse. The result was the Child Abuse Prevention and Treatment Act (CAPTA) of 1974. Its sponsors emphasized that child abuse cuts across all lines of race and class, which is true, and therefore appeared to be taking a color-blind perspective.

In the early 1970s, there was increasing public awareness of child abuse, and CAPTA was one result of this rising awareness. CAPTA lumped child *abuse* and *neglect* into an umbrella category of child *maltreatment*. In the process, CAPTA obscured the relationship of race and poverty to allegations of neglect, which account for the vast majority of state interventions into families.[16] CAPTA sets up a "treatment model" for child maltreatment, which essentially conflates the categories.

Marion Wright Edelman, who has been a powerful voice expressing the connections between race, systemic poverty, and child welfare, described the dilemma for progressives and liberals in responding to the backlash. "Because we recognized that support for whatever was labeled black and poor was shrinking . . . new ways had to be found to articulate and respond to the continuing problems of poverty and race."[17]

For many, the "new way" involved removing any discussion of race and racialized poverty from policy advocacy, and emphasizing treatment and rehabilitation. The effect is to obscure the institutional racism in which poverty and its consequent problems for children are rooted, and to focus on the perceived failures and pathology of people caught up in the system.

So, in a typical case, a parent doesn't need childcare; she needs parenting classes. She doesn't need affordable housing or a living wage or adequate income for quality food; she needs budgeting help and nutrition training. If she disagrees with the treatment plan, she's in denial and needs counseling, and if she *vehemently* disagrees, she may need anger management classes. If there's something she really *does* need, like addiction treatment, it may not be available without a long wait, and it may be in a program that can't accommodate parents. Her reward if she does everything right is to be described as "compliant," giving her a better chance of getting her kids back.

One writer, Tina Lee, an anthropologist who studied the child welfare system among parents and workers in New York City, discussed the importance of "performing compliance" as a metric of progress.[18] Lee found that workers had no way to measure fitness as a parent, often because the services didn't match up to the problems that brought the parent to the attention of the child welfare system in the first place. If the problem was unsafe housing or lack of childcare, completion of a parenting class does nothing to solve it. Attendance can be measured, however, and reported to a judge. Even if the problems are more closely related to the parent's behavior, such as substance abuse or domestic violence, measuring progress is difficult and subjective, so compliance with assigned program tasks is used. Lee found that workers also cited compliance with demands as a demonstration that parents were "serious" about getting their children back. The power to label a parent "noncompliant" is considerable, and parents and workers are aware of that.

There was a renewal of interest in preserving and reunifying families in legislation passed in 1980, the Adoption Assistance and Child Welfare Act. In design, the law was supposed to put greater effort into preventing removals and expediting returns or adoption—addressing the inertia of "foster care drift" that keeps children in foster care for years or until adulthood. The reunification/prevention requirements, however, were simply imposed on the treatment model, and the relationship between foster care and racialized poverty was not acknowledged.

The system maintained a color-blind perspective that continued to blame parents, a rising percentage of whom were Black, for being poor. The war on drugs and the HIV/AIDS epidemic put more and more kids into care, and—as mentioned—the response under Clinton included ASFA, which essentially said that "permanency" (defined as leaving foster care for reunification with parents, adoption, or guardianship by a relative) trumps family preservation. There are financial incentives to encourage adoption, and to encourage agencies to "free" children and finalize adoption. Nevertheless, many kids don't want to be adopted, and others linger in foster care because of a lack of adoptive parents.

Disproportionality in Foster Care

Race correlates with involvement in the child welfare system more closely than poverty.[19] While there are local variations, Latino children are not overrepresented in foster care, while the percentage of African American and Native American children in foster care is double that of their percentage of the general child population. Whites represent a significantly lower percentage than they do in the general child population, while Asian American children are the least likely to enter care. Since 40 percent of Black children and 34 percent of Latino children in 2012 lived in poverty,[20] the differences between Black and Latino representation in foster care indicates that while the foster care system is populated by poor families, race operates as a factor not wholly dependent on poverty.

The seminal work on race in foster care is Dorothy Roberts's book, *Shattered Bonds: The Color of Foster Care*, which is to child welfare what Michelle Alexander's *The New Jim Crow* is to mass incarceration. Roberts connects the penal and child welfare systems, when she writes:

> Considering the impact of incarceration on Black families reveals a relationship between the child welfare system and the criminal justice system. The most direct connection is that imprisoning parents throws many children into foster care. But there are other less obvious and more profound systemic associations between criminal justice and child welfare. Demographically, the two institutions are remarkably similar. They are both populated almost exclusively by poor people, and by grossly disproportionate numbers of Blacks.[21]

Roberts also makes the point that the spatial concentration of state intervention means that in neighborhoods like Mott Haven or Central Harlem in New York, or West Lawndale in Chicago, the extraordinarily high numbers of Black males in state custody or subject to state control through the criminal justice system is accompanied by a similar concentration of children in custody and women and families subject to state control through the child welfare system.[22] One more link is the gross overrepresentation of foster care alumni in juvenile justice facilities and penal institutions.

The long-term consequences of overrepresentation may include increased risk of poor educational outcomes as a result of being labeled with "serious emotional disturbance" (SED). If a child acts up after being taken from his or her home and put into care, the behavior may be said to be a product of the pathological home environment. Children in foster care are far more likely to be medicated and pushed into classrooms for kids with SED than the general school-age population.[23] A bonus for labeling the child is that the foster parent and agency may be entitled to a higher rate for foster care, meaning that the amount available ostensibly for the benefit of the child is much greater when he or she is in care than it ever was or will be with the child at home.

The overrepresentation of children in foster care among those given the SED label is extremely relevant to race. Just as Black children are significantly overrepresented in foster care, Black students are significantly overrepresented in special education, and the disproportionality is particularly acute among those classified with SED.[24] Furthermore, this overlapping tangle of disproportionality needs to be studied further, as disproportionate foster care placement may contribute to disproportionate placement in SED programs in school.

While the disproportional representation of Black children in foster care is undeniable, there has been a backlash among some academics, commenters, and policy makers about ascribing any role to institutional racism. A special report on foster care in Los Angeles by the *Inland Valley Daily Bulletin*, a newspaper in the Los Angeles metropolitan area, began with the revelation that Black children were 8 percent of the Los Angeles County's general child population, but comprised 29 percent of its foster care census.[25] That's not a surprising statistic, but the report went on essentially to make the case that racism has no real relevance.

The report describes Roberts as "one of a host of child welfare experts who during most of the 2000s believed that institutional racism was the leading cause of the high numbers of black children in foster care, an argument that has lost steam in the last few years in the face of new data." The work of Roberts and others is first oversimplified, as an attempt to blame "institutional racism and bias by social workers" for disproportional placement. Then it is dismissed on the basis that "the number of black children in foster care is almost identical to the percentage of black social workers," meaning that, "if racism is a factor, then the racism would come from a staff made up mostly of ethnic minorities."[26] The argument conflates *institutional* racism inherent in the foster care system with self-mediated bigotry and bias by individuals employed within the system. Having done so, it assumes that if the individuals are unlikely to bring racist attitudes into the system, the system as a whole must be free of racism.

The Los Angeles County report cites the Fourth National Incidence Study of Abuse and Neglect (NIS-4), which found that maltreatment of Black children occurs at about 1.7 times the national average. The problem with that statistic, however, is that it doesn't measure child maltreatment; it measures *reported* child maltreatment. The NIS-4 employed a "sentinel survey methodology," meaning that it surveys "community professionals who work in certain categories of agencies and who typically encounter children and families in the course of their job duties." These professionals "serve as lookouts for victims of child abuse and neglect," and they are found "in police and sheriffs' departments, public schools, day care centers, hospitals, voluntary social service agencies, mental health agencies, the county juvenile probation and public health departments, public housing, and shelters for runaway and homeless youth and for victims of domestic violence."[27]

One factor contributing to disproportionality is the far greater frequency Black families will interact with many of these sentinels. Another is the likelihood that "sentinels"—perhaps unconsciously—will be more vigilant lookouts when interacting with Black families in these settings. An additional factor is explicitly set out in the NIS-4 as an explanation for growth in the gap between NIS surveys. "Income, or socioeconomic status, is the strongest predictor of maltreatment rates, but since the time of the NIS–3, incomes of Black families have not kept pace with the incomes of White families."[28]

The analysts tried to control for factors other than race to explain the racial disparity, but found it difficult to do so, and urged that the data be "interpreted with caution," a warning that was clearly ignored in the case of the Los Angeles County investigation. How families are perceived by "sentinels," which parts of the network of lookouts they are coming into contact with, and the persistence of poverty for Black Americans are all beyond the NIS-4 "multi-factor" analysis.

Much of the "new data" the Los Angeles County report cites in support of its "race doesn't matter" thesis simply correlates poverty and associated risk factors (low birth weight, for example) to placement in foster care. Separating race and poverty, however, takes the child welfare system out of the context in which it operates.

The impulse to do so has some powerful voices. As noted earlier, Elizabeth Bartholet has made a career out of essentially denying that race is an issue in child welfare. She says, "The bottom line is that there is absolutely no evidence of system bias. What we do have is overwhelming evidence that there are higher black maltreatment rates." Bartholet's work has had more influence than an "exposé" in a regional newspaper ever will. In *Nobody's Children* (1999), she argues that reform means "freeing" children for adoption much faster and more readily, which means quickly abandoning efforts to preserve bonds with parents she deems inferior.

Bartholet also claims the mantle of feminism to justify devaluing the bonds between Black mothers and their children. As Dorothy Roberts notes, "Bartholet explicitly argues that this effort to separate black mothers from their children is feminist because the demand by the battered women's movement that the state 'punish male perpetrators and liberate their female victims' supports a similarly coercive approach to child abuse and neglect."[29] By likening Black mothers to batterers, Bartholet suggests that these mothers have complete responsibility for their children being in care, despite the fact that the circumstances may have included factors beyond their control, such as homelessness and poverty, or that may touch any family, such as alcohol or drug abuse, although white parents are less likely to get caught up in the child welfare system as a result. Bartholet portrays Black mothers as a threat to their children, unworthy of efforts to help and reunite the family.

The echoes of the mind-set that led to the Orphan Trains, Indian boarding schools, and educational planning for "Freedom's Children" are unmistakable, but Bartholet is also very much in step with the policy makers behind ASFA's push for "a quicker path to permanency," with an emphasis on adoption. In effect, overrepresentation of Black children is seen as evidence by Bartholet and others that Black parents are simply more likely to maltreat their children. The policy response is a "color-blind" system that ignores race generally and disproportionality in particular and concentrates on removing barriers to adoption.

The denial that institutional racism is relevant to disproportional representation serves a purpose. It makes it easier to separate the foster care system from its environment. An economic order that consigns 40 percent of Black children to poverty will necessarily overrepresent Black children in foster care. When policy makers limit their consideration to obvious bias within the foster care system itself—essentially redefining the term "institutional racism" out of existence—it makes it easier to tolerate the status quo.

The alternative, obviously, is to recognize that confronting overrepresentation in foster care means confronting the importance of race in the development and maintenance of capitalism. Because racism cannot be defended logically, there is a natural tendency to see it as a primitive ideology born of ignorance that has unfortunately survived in humankind. In actuality, however, the construct of "race" as a set of categories into which people could be sorted and assigned value arose with the dawn of capitalism.

Capitalism and Race

The precapitalist world certainly recognized divisions. Those considered "others" might be "savages" or "infidels." They might be conquered, enslaved, or massacred. They were not, as a rule, defined by a fixed category based on presumed biological inferiority.

Shakespeare's Othello was North African and Shakespeare made some metaphorical use of the darkness of his skin foreshadowing the darkness of his fate, but it's very difficult for a modern reader to recognize in the characters the concept of an African race—or for that matter a "white" race—that developed within a century following the first performance of the play for a popular audience at the beginning of the seventeenth century. Othello is superior in intellect, courage, and achievement to most of the other characters in the play, and Othello's tragic flaws, which the villainous Iago takes advantage of to destroy him, are universal and not based on any racial categorization.

The modern construct of race (and with it racism as a system of belief in the superiority of "white" over "black") really emerged as the Atlantic slave trade developed. As the historian Eric Williams stated, "Slavery was not born of racism; rather, racism was the consequence of slavery."[30] Racism as a system of belief was necessary to explain slavery as a basis for capital accumulation, different quantitatively and qualitatively from slavery as seen throughout the world previously.

In the US context, W. E. B. Du Bois argued:

> The espousal of the doctrine of Negro inferiority by the South was primarily because of economic motives and the interconnected political urge necessary to support the slave industry. . . The South could say that the Negro, even when brought into modern civilization, could not be civilized, and that, therefore, he and other colored peoples of the world were so far inferior to the whites that the white world had a right to rule mankind for their own selfish interests.[31]

As Du Bois explains, a belief in white superiority provided a justification not just for slavery, but for the conquest of indigenous people all over the world. It serves the further purpose for capitalism of dividing workers. As Frederick Douglass wrote, referring to exploited white wage-earners and more grossly exploited enslaved Blacks: "They divided both to conquer each. Both are plundered by the same plunderers. The slave is robbed by his master, of all his earnings above what is required for his physical necessities, and the white man is robbed by the slave system, because he is flung into competition with a class of laborers who work without wages."[32]

After emancipation, racist ideology served capital's purpose by helping to perpetuate the hyper-exploitation of Black wage laborers, which in turn helped to divide the working class into Black and white and suppress wages generally. As Sharon Smith notes, "Racism against Blacks and other racially oppressed groups serves both to lower the living standards of the entire working class and to weaken workers' ability to fight back. Whenever capitalists can threaten to replace one group of workers with another—poorly paid—group of workers, neither group benefits."[33]

Remembering that Marx identified the value of labor power as including not just the sustenance of laborers but their replenishment and replacement by the next generation of workers—the reproduction of labor power—we can see that the role of racism under capital will extend into social reproduction as well. We will explore this concept more fully in chapter 11.

At the dawn of capitalism, the enslaved Black worker began with no control over his or her labor. The racist ideology on which the system depended could allow no control over the reproduction of labor either, and, as we have seen, family life served as an important catalyst for resistance. The end of slavery did not mean that Black workers would be given the same level of discretion as white workers in the reproduction of their labor power. The continued importance of racist ideology, and the need to maintain heightened oppression for Black workers, meant that greater control would be exerted over Black family life than was deemed necessary to reproduce white labor power.

Thus, racism had to be incorporated into the various institutions developed to control Black youth and prepare them for the role capitalism reserved for them. This has included the sharecropping system and public education, as well as the child welfare and juvenile justice systems. Institutional racism in foster care, therefore, has little to do with subjective bias brought into the system by caseworkers and everything to do with the roots of the system and capitalism's continuing interest in controlling Black families and children.

"Killing the Indian to Save the Child"—Native American Children in Foster Care

Like Black children, indigenous children in the United States are represented in foster care at about double their percentage of the population of US children. Nationally, that means that indigenous children are 1 percent of the child population, but 2 percent of the foster care census. There are concentrations and tremendous variations, however. In Minnesota, indigenous children are represented at ten times their percentage of the child population, and in Alaska more than three times.[34]

Removal of Native American children and placement outside their tribe has a long and ugly history, and is charged with the genocidal intent of extinguishing the culture, traditions, and language of Native American children. Once the United States had largely succeeded in driving Native Americans off their tribal lands, by which time the indigenous population had been reduced by many millions, it turned to eradicating tribal life. Even the head of the US Bureau of Indian Affairs (BIA) was forced to acknowledge in 2000 that the BIA had practiced "ethnic cleansing" against tribes in the western United States.[35] One institution created to destroy these cultures was the Indian boarding school. Richard Pratt, an army officer who founded the first of the boarding schools, famously described the aim as being to "kill the Indian and save the man."

In 1878, an official from the BIA reasoned: "It must be manifest to all practical minds that to place these wild children under the teacher's care but four or five hours a day, and permit them to spend the other nineteen in the filth and degradation of the village, makes the attempt to educate and civilize them a mere farce."[36]

Nearly one hundred schools were created based on Pratt's method of "assimilation by total immersion." Children were punished for speaking native languages, and were subjected to instruction highlighting the superiority of white American culture to Indian life. The assimilation mission persisted into the 1960s.[37]

In the 1950s, the BIA and the Child Welfare League of America (CWLA), the premier professional association in child welfare, began collaborating on the Indian Adoption Project. Aggressive removals justified only by the poverty of the parents led to expedited adoptions, 85 percent by non-Native couples. In 2001, CWLA publicly apologized for its role in the project.[38]

In the early 1970s, about one third of indigenous children removed from their parents were still being placed in schools and institutions away from their tribes. Native peoples fought for the Indian Child Welfare Act (ICWA), passed by Congress in 1978, which gave tribes and Native parents the right to intervene in child welfare cases involving Indian children.

While ICWA was a victory for indigenous people brought about through struggle, states routinely ignore tribes in making removals and placements. ICWA puts the burden on tribes to enforce their rights by intervening in cases. Tribes with a dispersed and impoverished membership will be the ones most likely to have the greatest number of children involved with the child welfare system, and adequate resources for enforcement of rights are not provided. In 2013, the Winnebago tribe reported having three caseworkers investigating sixty-one cases in four states.[39] ICWA has not been tremendously effective at preventing the placement of indigenous children outside their tribes.

In a 2013 case known as the Baby Veronica case, the US Supreme Court began to roll back ICWA, in holding that a noncustodial Cherokee father could not prevent his daughter from being adopted by a white couple. The court said allowing the father to "play his ICWA trump card at the eleventh hour" would harm "vulnerable children" because "many prospective adoptive parents would surely pause before adopting any child who might possibly qualify as an Indian under the ICWA."[40] In other words, some children might lose the benefit of being adopted by a white couple if ICWA was not weakened.

The Supreme Court's decision was preceded by media coverage critical of ICWA for prioritizing tribal heritage over the best interests of children, as if the child's heritage is a matter of no importance to her. The *New York Times* headlined a 2013 story about the Baby Veronica case, "Focus on Preserving Heritage Can Limit Foster Care for Indians."[41] This followed an appearance in 2012 by the white couple seeking to adopt the child on the popular *Dr. Phil Show*. The show's host, Phil McGraw, misstated facts and presented the white couple and the child as victims of an unreasonable statute and a selfish father and tribe.[42]

Neither the *Times* nor McGraw made any reference to the ICWA's historical context, with out-of-home placement being used as a means of ethnic cleansing against indigenous tribes. If they were aware, they presumably thought it was irrelevant today. Nor did they mention the fact that ICWA—far from being a source of oppressive force wielded against powerless white couples—is actually ineffective at preventing the separation of indigenous children from their tribal cultures.

"LET ALL THAT IS INDIAN WITHIN YOU DIE"†
Recognizing America's Brutal Legacy
with Native American Families

By Judge William Thorne as told to Antoinette Robinson

Shortly after I started working as a tribal judge, one of my cases involved whether to remove children from their family. I didn't know much about the child welfare system and I needed to do some research. But I also trusted that the child welfare system knew the answers. The more I researched, though, the more I learned that the system was broken.

Since the 1880s, the United States government has been removing Native American children at high rates. That's when the Bureau of Indian Affairs began gathering Native American children up and taking them to boarding schools where the goal was to strip away the children's Indian identity. Children could have their mouths washed out with soap for speaking their tribal language. Some of the welcoming speeches recorded from when students arrived at the schools include the words: "Let all that is Indian within you die."

Children as young as four years old were taken to these schools. These were incredibly harsh places for children to be. The children had almost no contact with their families. In the first forty years of these schools, almost half of the children died, sometimes from disease, sometimes from broken hearts. They'd just stop eating. Often families were never informed that their children had died. They just never heard from them again. Some of these schools continued to exist right up to the 1980s.

A Wave of Removals

The worst part is that generation after generation of Native American children never had a parent pick them up and comfort them when they were sad, or cheer for them when they did well. They learned to be parents from matrons in the dormitories. Then those children became parents. But it's difficult to know how to hold a child if you've never been

---

† Reprinted with permission from *Rise*, a magazine written by parents affected by the child welfare system: www.risemagazine.org. This story appeared in the Fall 2014 issue of *Rise*.

held. It's difficult to know how to get down on the floor and play if it was never done with you.

Also, in the mid-1950s, the Child Welfare League of America and the Bureau of Indian Affairs started removing Indian children and placing them in non-Indian homes on charges of "neglect." In Indian communities, older children are often responsible for taking care of younger children— three- and four-year-olds might be in the care of eight- or nine-year-olds, but this became grounds for removal. By the early 1960s, 25–35 percent of all Native American children had been removed from their homes and put in foster or adoptive homes.

If the system had known what kind of home I grew up in, my brothers and sisters and I would have been removed. But if I'd been removed, I would have missed the opportunity to spend summers with my grandmother. My grandmother cooked on a wood stove. She had an outhouse, not a bathroom, and she didn't have spare bedrooms for us to sleep in. But my grandmother made me feel special. If I had been removed from my home, I might never have had that opportunity, and I wouldn't be who I am.

A Protective Law

In 1970, the United States Congress created the American Indian Policy Review Commission. It found that in some states Native American children were placed in foster care as much as twenty times more often than other children. That report was issued in 1977. In 1978, Congress passed the Indian Child Welfare Act (ICWA), which was an attempt to try to fix the problem.

ICWA requires child welfare systems to make "active efforts" to solve the problem before a child is removed. (In non-ICWA cases, the legal standard is lower—"reasonable efforts.") ICWA also gave preference to placing children with kin and moved some child welfare decisions back to tribal courts.

Change, But Not Enough

Now, thirty-five years later, fewer Native American children enter foster care. Some states have formed partnerships with tribes. In California, for instance, there is a good state judge–tribal judge partnership that meets together regularly to educate each other. In Utah and Washington states, cases involving Native American children are staffed together with both a state judge and a tribal judge. Some states also make an aggressive effort to place children with family whenever possible.

But we still see Native American children enter foster care in very high numbers. Nationally, a Native American child is two and a half times more likely to be in care than a non-Native child. In Minnesota, a Native American child is fourteen times more likely to be in care.

In many places, the barriers to tribal court involvement are distance and inadequate funding—tribal courts are working with only about a quarter of the resources of state courts. And even though ICWA holds child welfare systems to a higher standard of "active efforts," many states have found ways around that, because the federal government doesn't regularly review whether states are in compliance with ICWA.

Too many people still believe they're saving children when they go into a home and take children out without spending time understanding the family or whether problems can be fixed. And there is still a lot of resentment in the Native American community—a feeling that a lot of people are trying to get Indian children away from Indian families.

'Is This Child Loved?'

As a judge, I've had to ask, "If these were my kids, would this plan be acceptable to me?" If each of us spent more time asking ourselves that question, I think we would do a much better job providing for other people's children.

I believe the federal government ought to be tracking and publishing how often children from different racial and ethnic groups go into care. If communities knew the numbers, they'd know how bad it is and demand change.

I also think the federal government should penalize states for being out of compliance with ICWA. If states knew they could lose millions of dollars, they'd spend more time fixing the problems.

States should work with local tribes to provide training to help caseworkers understand tribal culture and history. I also believe there are too many formal licensing requirements when it comes to placing children with family. The questions we have to ask are: "Is this child loved and taken care of and safe?" Everything else—like how many rooms are in the house and whether the family members have met the official licensing standards—is a misdirection.

Fighting for Change

In the past two years, some tribes have been fighting for control over all child welfare decisions involving Native American children. In the past, federal foster care dollars (called Title IV-E funds) were not made available to tribes. Instead, it was up to individual states to decide how much to involve the tribes. Congress passed a correction to that two years ago, and there are now a couple of tribes that are receiving federal funds to run their own systems, with a handful of others being considered.

I believe the most important change the child welfare system has to make is to really understand that foster care is not neutral. Too often, the child welfare system acts like children are the equivalent of potted plants that you can move from a windowsill in one house to another windowsill in another house and they'll do just fine. But kids don't do that. What we know from brain science research is that the trauma of broken attachments can literally prevent children's brains from growing, and if you miss that growth opportunity, you can never go back and make that up.

CHAPTER 3

Parents with Disabilities

Poverty, Disability, and Child Welfare

Perhaps no group of parents face a greater threat of losing their children than parents with disabilities. First, building on a long history that has deliberately interfered with reproduction by the disabled through means that have included forced sterilization and long-term institutionalization, the child welfare and disability service systems continue to discriminate against people with disabilities based on a presumption of unfitness.

Second, people with disabilities experience poverty and unemployment at far higher rates than their non-disabled peers. In 2014, the poverty rate for individuals ages eighteen to sixty-four with disabilities was 28 percent, more than double the rate for adults without disabilities in the same age group.[1] That same year, only 34 percent of adults with disabilities were employed, compared to 75 percent of non-disabled adults.[2] The median earnings for an individual with a disability ages sixteen and up was roughly $21,000, more than a third less than the median earnings for individuals without disabilities.[3]

Since poverty subjects a parent to greater scrutiny and makes her vulnerable to allegations of neglect based in whole or in part on lack of material resources, it is to be expected that people with disabilities will come to the attention of the system frequently. Once scrutinized, there is an opportunity for biases against people with disabilities as parents to be brought into decision-making.

According to a 2012 study by the National Council on Disability (NCD), people with all categories of impairment experience discrimination when they attempt to parent, but state intervention occurs most frequently with parents who have psychiatric diagnoses or intellectual disabilities. Reliable national data doesn't exist, but NCD found local estimates that 70 to 80 percent of parents with psychiatric diagnoses and 40 to 80 percent of parents with intellectual disabilities have their children removed at some point.[4]

All disability classifications are affected, however. NCD found cases where newborns were removed directly from the hospital simply on the basis of a mother's disability without attempting to assess whether she was capable of caring for the child, with or without support.

Capitalism and Disability

Before looking at the origins and basis for discrimination against parents with disabilities, we should look at the role of capitalism in the creation of "disability" itself. Impairments of various kinds have obviously existed since the beginning of human society, and people with impairments experienced exclusion and/or violence throughout history, either because of some kind of superstition or because others felt they could not contribute to generating subsistence. But putting people with a wide range of impairments into a category of "disabled" is a modern phenomenon. Most activists against disability oppression adhere to a "social model of disability," and there is variation in how that model is described. Its most basic elements, however, are that "disability" is broader than impairment and is socially created. Impairment is something that affects the operation of a limb, organ, or body system; it may change the way one works or functions in daily life, and it may limit one's activities. For example, blindness, cerebral palsy, and intellectual disability are all impairments that affect life activities. Disability, however, is how an individual with an impairment is restricted in opportunity, rights, and resources because of the impairment. So a child with a visual impairment is affected in how she learns, and may require different teaching methods and resources than a child with typical vision. The impairment becomes a disability, however, when she is given an inferior education in a segregated environment, with limitations imposed on outcomes and opportunities. British writers and activists Michael Oliver and Colin Barnes describe the process as "social disablement."

> All people with impairments experience disability as social restriction, whether those restrictions occur as a consequence of inaccessible built environments, questionable notions of intelligence and social competence, the inability of the general public to use sign language, the lack of reading material in Braille or hostile attitudes to people with non-visible conditions and impairments. It's important to note that not all impairments have obvious functional limitations . . . what is considered an impairment is both materially and culturally determined.[5]

Oliver and Barnes argue that "it was the coming of capitalism that created disability as an individual problem."[6] They drew on earlier work by Victor Finkelstein, who described people with impairments in pre-industrial Britain who were thoroughly integrated into society, although usually at the bottom of the social hierarchy with the poor and unemployed. They were generally able to engage in some kind of economic activity in an agricultural and cottage-based economy, even if it was begging. This is not an idealized view of the precapitalist past; people with impairments generally shared the misery of the lowest orders of society. They did not, however, have a particular form of misery carved out for them as a class. No need for organized segregation as a class was seen until production began to be standardized, with labor being sold for wages—"large-scale industry with production lines geared to able-bodied norms."[7]

The response to the economic transformation of wage labor and industrial production was the creation of a separate class of individuals defined as a social problem, who had to be segregated and "sheltered." In addition to being thought incapable of conforming to the needs of the labor market, people with impairments might require care and attention, reducing the availability of family members for paid labor. Industrialization and urbanization, therefore, led to the development of asylums and custodial institutions in which the disabled could be segregated. Professions developed to classify people into different categories of disability based on ostensibly scientific diagnostic criteria—for example, "moral imbecility," and "involutional melancholia." Standardized intelligence testing and diagnostic schemes promised consistent terminology and helped to legitimize the professionals who administered the tests and applied the labels. The professions, and the institutions they developed and depended on, acquired power of their own to reinforce the idea that segregation was necessary and beneficial to people with disabilities.

Institutionalization of the "Feeble-Minded"

The first institutions built for people who today would be described as having intellectual disabilities, but who were then called "feeble-minded," were set up by educators, who envisioned them as schools preparing youth for some kind of productive activity back in the community. As the institutions matured, and the earliest residents became adults who could not be accommodated outside the institutions, the schools became long-term custodial hospitals, under the supervision of doctors rather than educators. While there was a material basis for these changes in the change in the relationship of labor to production, it had important ideological implications, by normalizing the idea that people with disabilities are a special class to be excluded from society for their own protection and society's betterment.[8]

The desire to suppress reproduction was particularly acute with regard to people with intellectual disabilities and psychiatric diagnoses. There was an assumption that these individuals would be unable to care for a child, especially if they did not measure up to an ideal of a self-sufficient nuclear family headed by adults who exchanged labor for money used to support children, and also performed all the work needed to care for themselves and their offspring. As will be discussed at greater length in chapter 11, the sale of labor in the marketplace is related to parenting because under capitalism, parents sell their labor for a wage that maintains them, and therefore sustains their ability to provide labor, but also supports their children, who will eventually join them and replace them in the workplace. This social reproduction function of the nuclear family under capitalism influences wage expectations as well as social policies relative to families.

The desire to prevent reproduction of people with intellectual disabilities and psychiatric diagnoses contributed to the expansion of institutions, as stays lengthened to ensure that people were locked up during what were presumed to be the childbearing years. That concern tended to be most focused on women, in part because of the recognition that women with mental disabilities in the community were sometimes vulnerable to sexual abuse, often while engaged in domestic labor, one of the only workplaces where they were accommodated. Others might engage in prostitution because they had no other employment options. Pregnancy and parenting was not acceptable for women who were defined as disabled, and institutionalization was one response. Sexual activity often happened in institutions, either as a result of consensual relationships or abuse, so institutionalization was not a complete solution. For one thing, pregnancy within the institution was disruptive of the smooth running of the facility. In an effort to contain the cost of the institutions, the inmates were assigned to work. Some farmed, and others worked in manufacturing within the facility. Ironically, given their supposed inability to care for children, women in facilities were often assigned to care for children committed at a young age or older inmates requiring personal care. Pregnancy and parenting would complicate the use of the inmate labor force.

Eugenics

During the period from about 1900 to 1920, as the institutional custodians dominated the field of disability policy making, theorists in various fields began to promote the ideology of "eugenics."[9] The term *eugenics* was coined in 1883 by a British scientist named Sir Francis Galton, and it draws on Greek roots meaning "well born." Galton defined it as "the study of all agencies under human

control which can improve or impair the quality of future generations." Galton was a cousin of Charles Darwin, and eugenics was
inspired in part by Darwin's theory of natural selection. It was the
belief that human evolution could be substantially influenced by a
scientific approach to breeding.

Initially, Galton's preoccupation was with the heredity of genius,
and he was most concerned with what became known as "positive
eugenics," the encouragement of scientific mate selection and more
prolific reproduction among the "higher" classes. Galton admitted to the possibility of "negative eugenics," the discouragement
of reproduction among those considered undesirable, but he said
that too little was known about heredity to develop or implement
eugenic controls on society. Unlike many later eugenicists, Galton
actually *was* a scientist, so he always emphasized that his theories
couldn't be proven. The American eugenicists who followed were
much bolder and more confident.

Two of the most important American eugenicists were Charles
Davenport, who advanced genealogical research to prove the inheritance of behavioral characteristics, and Harry Laughlin, who was
a sort of promoter and lobbyist. Both worked out of Carnegie-
supported institutions in Cold Spring Harbor on Long Island.
Davenport got prison officials, state hospitals, welfare departments, and other public institutions to turn over their records, and
US Consular offices overseas cooperated with genealogical studies
of applicants for immigration visas. The government was riddled
with supporters of eugenics, and at least four successive presidents
from Theodore Roosevelt to Warren Harding were among them.
Laughlin, for his part, promoted model legislation against interracial marriage and for involuntary sterilization. He also advised
on immigration restrictions in the 1920s, and was instrumental in
getting bills passed that enshrined discrimination based on country
of origin. That was the only federal legislation the eugenicists ever
got, and it fell far short of what they wanted. They were, however,
successful in getting states to pass laws against interracial marriage
and allowing for the compulsory sterilization of people with certain
categories of disability.

Instead of focusing on the breeding of geniuses, the US branch of eugenics was much more concerned with preventing the breeding of the "feeble-minded." Symptoms of feeble-mindedness included chronic pauperism, sexual immorality (primarily for women), sexual deviance (generally in the form of same-sex attraction), behavioral difficulties among children, alcohol abuse, and a variety of physical characteristics thought to be correlated to feeble-mindedness. The people who were scrutinized for these symptoms were poor and working class, and disproportionately immigrants or the children of immigrants, or poor rural whites. Some later manifestations of eugenics, including some contemporary policies that have been described as neo-eugenics, were directed almost exclusively against women of color, but in its earliest days eugenics was concerned with "purifying" the white race, and in the case of sterilization was carried out on an institutionalized population. Blacks were concentrated in southern states and excluded from most institutions in the South, so they weren't targeted for eugenic sterilization until later, when the rationale had shifted from inheritance to dependency and the cycle of poverty.

The first law providing for involuntary sterilization was passed in Indiana in 1907, but it was only used for a short time before a moratorium was imposed and it was declared unconstitutional in 1921. Other states passed laws, but there was doubt about their constitutionality, so sterilization was practiced on a limited scale until after the Supreme Court upheld Virginia's statute in 1927. That case, known as *Buck v. Bell*, did not come about by happenstance.[10] The law was carefully drafted to minimize vulnerability to constitutional challenge, and the individual to be a plaintiff in a test case was also selected very purposefully. Carrie Buck was a young woman labeled "feeble-minded," although she had gotten good grades in school, so it's not clear that she had any kind of impairment. Her mother had been arrested for prostitution in the past and was herself institutionalized. Carrie was working as a servant in a home when she was raped by the nephew of the couple she worked for. The crime was covered up, and when she got pregnant, her employers had her committed to an institution for the feeble-minded. All this was known to the custodian of the institution, but it was kept out of the record of the case. Carrie gave birth to a little girl, who was placed in foster care in the home in which Carrie had been raped. The choice of a family represented by three generations was no accident, and it's probable that the selection of three generations of females was also no accident. A lawyer was appointed for Carrie, but he was in collusion with the state to lose so that the case could go to the Supreme Court, where he did his best to lose as well. The state asserted that Carrie's baby was also feeble-minded, and the courts accepted that even though the only evidence was a social worker who testified that the baby "didn't seem quite normal." When it reached the Supreme Court, Oliver Wendell Holmes, still considered one of the intellectual giants of the court, wrote the majority opinion upholding Virginia's sterilization statute. He wrote in part:

> Carrie Buck is a feebleminded white woman who was committed to the State Colony . . . she is the daughter of a feebleminded mother in the same institution, and the mother of an illegitimate feebleminded child. . . . It is better for all the world, if instead of waiting to execute degenerate offspring for crime, or to let them starve for their imbecility, society can prevent those who are manifestly unfit from continuing their kind. The principle that sustains compulsory vaccination is broad enough to cover cutting the Fallopian tubes. Three generations of imbeciles are enough.

Buck v. Bell opened up the floodgates for coercive sterilization. States could copy the model legislation used by Virginia, and many did. Sterilizations increased dramatically. About thirty states ended up with legislation. There was opposition from Catholics, especially after Pope Pius XI issued an encyclical opposing eugenic sterilization in 1930, and many of the states in which sterilization bills failed had large or influential Catholic populations. In some states, bills were passed but used sparingly. Some states were very enthusiastic about sterilization. California alone sterilized about a third of the approximately sixty thousand people sterilized nationally by about 1970. Most of those sterilized were women, and in some states women made up as high as 60 to 80 percent of those sterilized. In a couple of states men were the majority, and in some it was roughly equal. Sterilization of men during this period and today is less intrusive, risky, and expensive than sterilization of women, so the fact that cost-conscious institutions overrepresented women to a significant degree seems to indicate that sterilization of women was a higher priority. So while eugenics was certainly directed against both working-class men and women with disabilities, there was a special fury directed toward women.

Sterilization statutes often targeted patients at psychiatric hospitals, but proved more difficult in practice because of greater resistance from patients and family, so sterilization of these populations was less common than people with cognitive disabilities. Statutes also provided for sterilization of prisoners, but in 1942 the Supreme Court said that sterilizing prisoners was a violation of due process, in contrast to the court's holding with regard to people with cognitive disabilities.

When the Nazis came to power, leadership of the eugenics movement, which they called "race hygiene," suddenly shifted to Germany. US eugenicists were both excited and jealous because the Nazis represented a national government with absolute power committed to eugenic policies, which eventually included extermination, starting with people with disabilities and moving on to Jews, gays, and other groups. Hitler expressed admiration for American eugenicists in *Mein Kampf* and elsewhere, and the Nuremberg Laws were modeled in part on American legislation drafted in Cold Spring Harbor and shopped around to state legislatures. In 1934, the superintendent of an institution in Virginia said publicly, "The Germans are beating us at our own game!" But as US opinion turned against the Nazi regime, lots of mainstream eugenicists and even more so their funders were left in an embarrassing position. Even the Rockefellers eventually stopped funding German eugenics institutions as the war approached. American eugenicists largely dropped the eugenics label after World War II, and migrated into the population control movement and, in some cases, genetic research.

"New-genics"

The eugenic sterilization of people with mental disabilities outlasted eugenics as a respectable ideology. State-initiated sterilization continued into the 1960s, and some laws were never repealed. Although these laws are not currently invoked, involuntary sterilization procedures and abortions still occur when parents or guardians, health care providers, public agencies—and sometimes the courts—agree. In 2007, doctors at Seattle Children's Hospital agreed with the parents of "Ashley," a young girl with developmental disabilities, on a new "collection of interventions" to prevent Ashley from growing or developing sexually. Claiming it would spare her pain in later life, they agreed to massive doses of hormones to keep her small, beginning when Ashley was six, followed by the removal of her breasts and a complete hysterectomy when she was nine. Her parents argued that she "wouldn't need" these organs later in life, and having them might "sexualize her to caregivers," making her vulnerable to abuse. The hospital's ethics committee agreed to allow the procedures. No court order was obtained, in apparent violation of state law. Disability advocates learned about it because two of the doctors wrote an article in a medical journal promoting what has become known as the "Ashley Treatment."[11] NCD reported that the Ashley Treatment had been used on more than one hundred other children.[12]

In Massachusetts in 2012, a judge granted the state's petition to appoint the parents of a thirty-two-year-old woman with psychiatric diagnoses to act as her guardians for the purpose of consenting to an abortion she had insisted she did not want. The judge specified in his order that they could coerce or trick their daughter, if necessary, to get the procedure performed. While he was at it, the judge also ordered that the girl be sterilized at the same time to prevent future pregnancy, even though neither the state nor the parents had asked for sterilization. On appeal, the order for sterilization was overturned, and the case was sent to another judge to determine whether the woman would agree to the abortion if she were "mentally competent." The parents continued to act as her guardians.[13]

Laws restricting the rights of people with psychiatric diagnoses to marry exist in thirty-three states, and twenty-seven restrict their parenting rights. Unlike the eugenic sterilization laws that linger on the books, many of these statutes are recent. Four states passed new laws during the 1990s.[14]

One reason for the persistence of eugenic practices long after the pseudo-scientific basis of inheritance of disability and behavioral characteristics had been rejected is that eugenic ideology always blended arguments about inheritance, capacity, and dependence. So while eugenic policies may no longer be justified on strict hereditary grounds, arguments are made that a person with a disability is unfit to parent, and that children will be a drain on public resources because the parents will be unable to support them.

While sterilization and coerced abortions occur outside the child welfare system, the continued power of eugenic ideas in society forms a backdrop for the discrimination against parents with disabilities that occurs in the system. As of 2005, thirty-seven states included disability as a factor in determining whether a parent's rights should be terminated after a finding of abuse or neglect. A termination of parental rights (TPR) proceeding is required in order for the child to be adopted. Most commonly specified were intellectual or developmental disabilities and psychiatric diagnoses, but a number of states included a category of "emotional illness" and five states included physical disabilities.[15] Rights are not supposed to be terminated because of the disability, but the disability is said to be evidence, along with behavior and lack of compliance, that makes the parent unfit as a parent. Listing the disability, however, focuses attention on the disability as a barrier to parenting rather than on supports and resources that can help the family function successfully.

Proceedings to terminate rights are also more likely to be "fast-tracked" for parents with disabilities. Ordinarily, states are required to make "reasonable efforts" to reunite the family by providing supports and services, and they have to demonstrate what efforts they have made in court, in order for a TPR proceeding to move forward. When it passed the Adoption and Safe Families Act (ASFA) in 1994, Congress loosened the requirement in cases involving extraordinary circumstances, such as a parent who has killed or seriously injured another of their children or who has seriously injured, sexually abused, or tortured the removed child. In the process of crafting these bypass provisions, Congress threw in an additional exception when they excused states from efforts at reunification if a parent had previously had rights terminated for another child. So if a parent with a disability previously had a child removed and could not get the child back because of lack of supports, the state would have to make no effort with any subsequent children. In addition, Congress created a catchall category of "aggravated circumstances," including torture and sexual abuse, and allowed states to add to the list of what constitutes aggravated circumstances. Six states include a parent's disability in their definitions of aggravated circumstance, allowing them to bypass reasonable efforts to reunify and instead move straight to TPR.[16]

Massachusetts was cited in a 2015 Letter of Findings from the US Departments of Justice and Health and Human Services for multiple civil rights violations in the case of a woman referred to in the letter by the pseudonym "Sara Gordon." Sara was a twenty-one-year-old woman with intellectual disability who was investigated by the Massachusetts Department of Children and Families (DCF) shortly after giving birth to a baby girl referred to as "Dana." DCF personnel acted under the assumption that Sara could not care for Dana because of her disability. For over two years, DCF ignored support services that could have been made available to Sara and Dana, and also ignored the supports they would be receiving from Sara's own parents. DCF was evaluating Sara based on her capacity to care for her child completely alone and without assistance. They also restricted Sara's visits with Dana, frustrating her efforts to develop a bond and become more proficient in providing care. In the Letter of Findings, DOJ and HHS wrote:

> DCF has continually asserted that Ms. Gordon poses a safety risk to Dana if she were to parent on her own, without consideration of any supports. However, DCF has ignored the fact that Ms. Gordon is not proposing to parent on her own without any supports, has ignored its own ability and obligation to provide

such supports, and has repeatedly ignored the objective evaluations of various clinical and service professionals (including the
majority of the most recent Foster Care Review panel) who have
reviewed this case and found that Ms. Gordon's plan to parent
Dana with her family's support is appropriate. Instead, DCF has
refused to reconsider the permanency plan for adoption and has
sought to terminate Ms. Gordon's parental rights.[17]

It's worth reflecting on what DCF's position says about the expectations for working-class parents under capitalism. The role of the
nuclear family is to provide all the care a child requires, and support
from extended family or community resources is not to be expected.
Thus, DCF felt justified in considering Sara Gordon's capacity as a
lone individual, and hold her need for support against her. There
are wealthy parents who never contemplate caring for their children
without the assistance of nannies and housekeepers, however, and
no assumption is made that they are incompetent as parents. They
are not expected to be able to cope with the hypothetical complete
absence of support because they are in a position to pay for it.

Discrimination in Disability Service Systems

Discrimination is by no means confined to the child welfare system. One of the problems for parents with disabilities, especially
those with intellectual disabilities or psychiatric diagnoses, is that
the same systems that actively restricted their right to parent for
generations are responsible for providing them with supports to live
full lives in the community. Disability service systems may no longer seek to institutionalize people for life, but neither do they accept
that they need to adapt community supports to meet the needs of
parents.

In one example with which I am personally involved, in New
York State the Office for People with Developmental Disabilities
(OPWDD) is responsible for services for people with intellectual
disabilities, which it generally does through contracts and billing
arrangements with nonprofit service providers. In order to qualify
for supportive housing, a person has to fit the definition of having

a developmental disability. So if a parent who would be eligible for supportive housing has a child who would not, OPWDD takes the position that it has no responsibility for the child, so the apartment has to be developed with a budget that includes only the parent. Since the housing cost would likely exceed the amount OPWDD would pay the service provider, almost none are willing to attempt to develop residences for parents who will be living with their children. Sometimes women are forced to leave supportive housing when they become pregnant, because they will not be able to bring the child home with them. Others who have children in care are unable to plan for reunification unless they give up their supportive housing. Often a woman will be discharged to family, but when things don't work out she may become homeless and enter the shelter system.

OPWDD also canceled a contract to provide parenting classes and support to parents with intellectual disabilities under a funding stream called "Family Support." One of several reasons they felt the program was inappropriate for the funding stream was that most of the parents had their children in foster care, so OPWDD took the bureaucratic position that they were "households of one" and therefore ineligible for Family Support. OPWDD allowed the program to continue by changing the funding stream to a different category using Medicaid funds, but this requires enrollees to complete a lengthy eligibility determination and enrollment process that can take months. There must be recent documentation of current level of functioning as well as evidence that the impairment began before age twenty-two. Even if it is obvious to clinicians and others that the impairment has been and will be lifelong, some kind of documentation must be tracked down or created. When parents are referred in the midst of a child welfare investigation, they likely need services quickly, but OPWDD does not accommodate that need because its focus is on the eligibility of the parent and not on the need of the family. This does not reflect a lack of concern on the part of the individuals within the bureaucracy, but the culture of a disability-specific agency that jealously guards its resources and takes pains to avoid expenditures to benefit someone who isn't "one of ours," which is a phrase I have heard used on a regular basis.

Service provider agencies are also resistant to adapting to meet the needs of families. Many of the largest are older charitable organizations, which are most responsive to the needs of families headed by nondisabled parents who are planning for the needs of a child with a disability. Traditionally, they have seen their role as preventing harm from coming to people with disabilities, not supporting them as they live self-directed lives in the community.

While my experience has been with parents with intellectual disabilities in New York City, the policies and attitudes I have seen are characteristic of the disability service system nationally. A few programs across the country advocate for parents with disabilities, including those involved with the child welfare system. One of the most successful has been Through the Looking Glass (TLG) in Berkeley, California. TLG was founded in 1982 by Hal and Megan Kirshbaum as part of the independent living movement, and their stated goals were "(1) to bring a disability culture perspective to early preventive intervention with families with disability/medical issues in infant/child or parent; and (2) to bring awareness about families and parenthood to the independent living community."[18] The independent living movement began in Berkeley around Ed Roberts, a man with physical disabilities who sued in 1962 for barrier-free access to the university, which had forced him to live in its infirmary.[19] As the political activity around Roberts matured into the national and international independent living movement, it was based on two broad principles, that all people with disabilities have a right to be included in all aspects of community life, and that individuals with disabilities need to have the power to make choices and have control over their own lives.[20]

Programs like TLG represent a break with traditional charitable organizations that were organized around a mission of helping the unfortunate. These organizations can in themselves be "disabling" in perpetuating the idea of helplessness and in imposing choices on people with disabilities. TLG is largely staffed by people with various impairments, and its mission is to fight alongside people with disabilities for the same right to parent—with appropriate supports—that people without disabilities have. TLG provides legal advocacy, support groups, peer mentoring, and a range of other supports.

Efforts to assert the rights of parents with disabilities have been scattered and local, and are generally focused on individual advocacy and systemic legal challenges. A handful of programs offer supports and parenting classes specifically designed for parents with impairments. These are absolutely vital, and need to be more widely replicated. Much more work, however, is needed to bring parents with disabilities into broader parent organizing.

LORENA'S STORY*

Lorena, an older Latina mother in California who has autism, has raised one daughter to adulthood. Her daughters Sasha and Marie—ages twelve and fourteen, respectively—still live with her. Lorena was unable to work for several years, and between her autism and Sasha's autism, the cost of treatment and transportation for medical, educational, and therapeutic care resulted in their becoming homeless. Lorena contacted social services for help. They convinced her to place Marie and Sasha in foster care temporarily. Because of Sasha's disability, she was placed separately from her big sister in a special needs foster care home. Lorena was very upset that her children were separated. Her case moved from voluntary to involuntary, and a public defender was appointed. Lorena became alarmed when she saw Sasha's deteriorating emotional state and lack of personal hygiene: long, jagged, dirty nails; unwashed hair; inflamed and infected gums. Child welfare workers reprimanded her for taking pictures of her daughter's condition and sending them to county counsel representing social services. When Lorena became overwhelmed and upset during a visit with Sasha because Marie was not brought, as had been promised, the police were called to intervene. They found no safety issue. Child welfare then required Lorena to submit to two psychological evaluations. If these evaluations were interpreted to show that Lorena was unlikely to benefit from parenting services, she could be bypassed (denied the due process rights that a nondisabled parent receives). Lorena "failed" the tests and was deemed bypassed, ending her limited services and visitation. Throughout this process, Lorena felt that her public defender was unmotivated to help. The attorney never raised the ADA, even to argue against bypass; was not willing to accommodate Lorena's communication needs; was dismissive of motherly concerns about her vulnerable daughter's care; and refused to work with [Through the Looking Glass]. Ultimately, however, the children's attorney became interested in working with TLG's legal program. Together, they located a psychiatrist affiliated

---

* Pseudonyms are used for all family members. This vignette was submitted by Through the Looking Glass to the National Council on Disability for the NCLD's report, *Rocking the Cradle: Ensuring the Rights of Parents with Disabilities and Their Children* (2012).

with a local university disability program who had research and clinical familiarity with the subject. Despite the bypass, the local child welfare agency agreed to fund a proper assessment.

CHAPTER 4

Foster Youth[1]

Trauma in Foster Care

In 2013, the House Ways and Means Committee held a hearing on child sex trafficking and the links to foster care. The context for the hearing included the fact that the same year the FBI had conducted coordinated raids in seventy cities, and found that 60 percent of the children they found being trafficked had been in foster care. A year earlier, Connecticut reported eighty-eight victims of child sex trafficking, eighty-six of whom had been in care or involved with the child welfare system.[2]

At the hearing, a young woman named Withelma "T" Ortiz Walker Pettigrew testified about why her experience as a foster child prepared her to be trafficked. She said:

> I spent, for the most part, the first eighteen years of my life in the foster care system. Seven of those years I was a child being sexually trafficked on the streets, Internet, strip clubs, massage parlors and even in the back of express papers. Many children, like myself, come from various traumas previously to entering into foster care, and many times, are further exposed to trauma throughout their experience in the foster care system. . . . Youth within the system are more vulnerable to becoming sexually exploited because youth accept and normalize the experience of being used as an object of financial gain by people who are supposed to care for us, we experience various people who control our lives, and we lack the opportunity to gain meaningful relationships and attachments. In addition, traffickers/pimps/exploiters have no fear of punishment

because they rely on the lack of attention that occurs when these young people go missing. . . . Many children, myself included, who grow up in foster care express how it is common household knowledge that many caregivers take them in primarily for the paycheck in which they are provided for the purpose of caring for the child. . . . These caregivers will make statements like "you're not my child, I don't care what's going on with you, as long as you're not dead, I'll continue to get my paycheck." This "nothing but a paycheck" theory objectifies the youth and the youth begin to normalize the perception that their presence is to be used for financial gain. This creates a mind frame for the youth that their purpose is to bring income into a household. . . . Therefore, when youth are approached by traffickers/pimps/exploiters, they don't see much difference between their purpose of bringing finances into their foster home and bringing money to traffickers/pimps/exploiters' "stable." . . .

Like me, any youth in foster care becomes accustomed to adapting to multiple moves from home to home, which allows us to easily then adapt to when traffickers/pimps/exploiters move us multiple times, from hotel to hotel, city to city, and/or state to state. For myself, as unfortunate as it is to say, the most consistent relationship I ever had in care was with my pimp and his family.[3]

It's common to attribute poor outcomes among foster youth to the trauma they experienced prior to entering the system, and in Ms. Walker Pettigrew's case, there was such trauma, and she was further traumatized while in care. She describes the lack of concern with her whereabouts and well-being from those charged with providing care, because so long as she fulfilled her function of bringing revenue into the household, the relationship was satisfactory for the caregivers. There is also the instability in relationships and physical location that makes adjusting to the life of a trafficked teen easier. But what is most remarkable in her testimony is her description of the manner in which she was prepared for the commodification she experienced when she was trafficked by commodification while in foster care.

The totality of Ms. Walker Pettigrew's experience with foster care is not representative of all children in care. Many experience stable, loving relationships with foster parents, and most do not spend their entire childhoods in the system. Many individuals working within the system recognize the traumatic effect of being in care, and do their best to minimize it. Nevertheless, the issues she describes—the trauma, abuse, neglect, and commodification—are common enough to be considered features of the system.

Again, our commonsense notion may tell us that removing a child from a situation at home where she is now experiencing trauma or at risk of trauma in the future means that she is at least protected from further trauma. The reality is that the removal itself generally inflicts trauma.[4] This is recognized universally within the field, but child protective workers are limited in their responses. They can't quickly remove the stressors that may increase the likelihood for maltreatment, which include homelessness or housing instability, lack of income, inconsistent or ineffective mental health treatment, lack of childcare, the combination of the lifestyle circumstances imposed by the criminalization of drug abuse and the scarcity of nonpunitive drug treatment, and a myriad of other environmental risk factors. If they could do so, they could vastly reduce the number of children removed for neglect and abuse. This would leave the system better equipped to respond to those remaining cases of physical, psychological, and sexual abuse and severe neglect that warrant removal. A system downsized in this manner would be better able to concentrate resources and attention to minimize the harm that is experienced by children as a result of being removed from their parents—whatever their frailties—and placed in the care of substitute parents. This harm may result from the trauma of removal and also from maltreatment in foster care.

Removal may be preventive, as evidenced by spikes in removals that sometimes occur after a high-profile child abuse fatality. There is a harm that *may* occur without removal, and workers are unable to risk being held accountable if it does. As a result, they make decisions that ensure that a different harm almost certainly *will* occur. One worker in Los Angeles County described a case involving children removed after a fatality involving a four-year-old sibling. The death followed an illness and was unexplained, but there was no indication of wrongdoing by any family member. Shortly thereafter, the mother fled with the youngest child and the father agreed to bring the remaining children to live with him in his parents' house. After six months, despite no evidence the father had done anything wrong, the children were removed from the grandparents and placed in care in several different homes. While with their grandparents, the children had done well in school and displayed typical behavior for their ages. Shortly after their removal and separation:

> The children started developing clinical-grade symptoms, such as depressed mood, markedly diminished interest or pleasure in almost all activities, insomnia, recurrent and distressing dreams, intrusive thoughts and images, fatigue or loss of energy, feelings of worthlessness, outbursts of rage, diminished ability to think or concentrate, hyper-vigilance, avoidance behaviors, feeling of detachment, acting or feeling as if the trauma were recurring or crying spells.[5]

In this case, faced with an unexplained fatality, the system functioned in self-protective mode. If the parent could not be proven to be blameless in causing the sibling's death, the children would be removed prophylactically, on the chance that something might happen for which the system would be blamed. As a result, the children displayed all the symptoms of post-traumatic stress. If anything, these symptoms would be a barrier to reunification, as the parent would be scrutinized to see if he had the strength and support to deal with children with emotional disturbance.

One thing that is indisputable is that children in foster care need support and care, and careful attention to their mental health as a consequence of what are now described as "adverse childhood experiences."[6] This is the case whether they have experienced trauma before, during, or after removal, or as is typical, multiple traumatic experiences during all three periods in their lives.

While it would be comforting to believe that removal into foster care at the very least is protection against abuse, this is not the case. A study of women who had been in foster care as children found that they were much more likely to report being subjected to sexual abuse during their time in care than prior to placement. They were slightly more likely to have experienced physical abuse or intimidation in foster care than previously.[7] Texas's system was thrown into turmoil when ten children in foster care, out of a foster care population of thirteen thousand, died from homicide in fiscal year 2013, meaning that the rate of fatalities from abuse was far higher for the foster care population than for children at home. The Texas legislature held hearings, but offered no solutions other than increased drug testing for foster parents.[8]

In 2016 in suburban Suffolk County on Long Island, a foster parent was arrested and indicted for physically and sexually abusing five children in his care. The foster parent had been investigated by police nine times previously, but charges had not been filed. Nevertheless, Suffolk County in 2002 instructed the foster care agency, SCO Family of Services, to stop placing children from Suffolk in the home. SCO also works with children in nearby New York City, and it never told the city's Administration for Children's Services about the directive from Suffolk County, although it was legally required to do so. As a result, SCO continued to place children in the home for another fourteen years, with at least a hundred children passing through the home. Once it learned about the arrest, ACS stopped making new placements through SCO, and initiated safety inspections of all homes monitored by SCO, which contained some five hundred children at any given time.[9]

Foster Care and the Mental Health Marketplace

Professionals seeking to provide support and assistance are limited by the need to conform to the norms of market-driven practice to provide treatment. To obtain Medicaid reimbursement for providing treatment, a provider must apply a diagnostic label from the *Diagnostic and Statistical Manual of Mental Disorders*, or DSM. In its current incarnation as the DSM-5, the book is the means by which the American Psychiatric Association maintains its lucrative monopoly on psychiatric "nosology"—the classification of diseases and disorders. Without an appropriate label, treatment is almost certainly unavailable.

One critic of the DSM is Gary Greenberg, a self-described "lunchbucket psychotherapist" and blogger, and the author of a book about the DSM-5 called *The Book of Woe*. Greenberg relates the story of a Louisiana physician named Samuel Cartwright who, in 1850, defined a new disease he called "drapetomania," which caused Black slaves to run away. The primary symptom was unhappiness about being a slave. In the modern context, if a child acts out in anger as a result of having experienced poverty, homelessness, and disruption among caregivers, he might be diagnosed with some DSM formulation of conduct disorder. The point Greenberg makes is that being dissatisfied with the social order and one's place in it is often pathologized because of "invisible prejudices and fallacies."

Greenberg's main problem with the DSM is the awesome power it gives to the diagnostician to "give a name to suffering," and thereby define the diagnosed individual. The point is similar to that of Paulo Freire in *Pedagogy of the Oppressed*, when he discussed the "power of naming." Freire writes, "To exist, humanly, is to name the world, to change it. . . . Because dialogue is an encounter among women and men who name the world, it must not be a situation where some name on behalf of others. It is an act of creation; it must not serve as a craft instrument for the domination of others."[10]

Once properly labeled, treatment can be provided, but treatment is focused not on the child or her suffering, but on the label. The act of diagnosis objectifies the child. Thereafter, the child is not speaking except as a representative of a diagnosis. We should not ascribe malicious motives to those who push the child through the diagnostic mechanisms within the system. Typically, they are seeking help for a child in distress, and the only way to provide support is through diagnosis. Properly documented diagnoses may offer a higher rate of payment for foster parents, which may be important in preventing placements from being disrupted. It may also offer assignment to workers with lower "special needs" caseloads and a greater ability to provide individualized attention and support.

A related phenomenon is the extraordinary rates at which children in foster care are prescribed psychotropic drugs, or drugs intended to affect brain processes and behavior. A 2011 Government Accountability Office report looked at five states (Texas, Michigan, Oregon, Florida, and Massachusetts) and using 2008 data found that children in foster care were substantially more likely to be prescribed psychotropics than non-foster children on Medicaid. In these five states alone, Medicaid spent some $376 million on psychotropic medication for children, and the percentage of children up to age seventeen in foster care prescribed psychotropics varied from about 20 percent to nearly 40 percent. This variation should be troubling, because if these prescribing practices are demonstrably valid, one would expect more or less consistent rates in different states. The study also looked at the percentage of children prescribed five or more psychotropic medications at the same time, the percentage prescribed a dosage exceeding the maximum on the FDA-approved labels, and the percentage of infants less than one year of age prescribed psychotropic drugs. Again, there was tremendous variability from state to state, but there was extraordinary disproportionality in each category for children in foster care.[11]

Given the very high rates at which children and youth in foster care are being prescribed medication, we shouldn't be surprised by data indicating that at least half of kids aging out of care have used illegal drugs, nor should we assume that this reflects the influence of birth parents or their home communities rather than the system that took responsibility for raising them.[12]

Again, we should not assume that psychiatrists and nurse-practitioners are callously pumping drugs into children without regard to the consequences. They are often placed in the position of being the last person the system turns to when a child's behavior makes institutionalization or disruption of placement likely. A foster parent desperate for help may turn to a foster care agency, saying that she cannot maintain the child in her home without some kind of intervention. The agency, knowing that another change of foster home may well aggravate the situation or trigger placement in an institutional setting, may turn to prescribing clinicians to solve the problem pharmacologically. The problem is not bad intentions, but the lack of resources and flexibility to address children's distress in better ways.

"Aging Out"

About twenty-eight thousand young people "age out" of foster care each year. These are the youth who have not achieved the elusive goal of permanency, in that they never left foster care to live with biological or adoptive parents or court-appointed guardians. Instead, they remained in foster care until the maximum age for their state, which can range from eighteen to twenty-one.

A longitudinal study that tracked aged-out youth in Illinois, Iowa, and Wisconsin found that at age twenty-six, 46.8 percent were unemployed (compared with 20 percent of a demographically representative control group). Of males, 81.8 percent had been arrested at some point in their lives, compared with 41 percent of the control group. The comparable figures for females were 59 percent and 14.8 percent. Some 31 percent had attended a year or more of college, but only 8.2 percent had a two-year degree or higher. Of those who had dropped out of a vocational program or college, 60 percent reported that financial barriers prevented them from continuing. The median annual income for the aged-out youth was $8,950, compared with $27,310 for the control group.[13] Data suggests that nearly half of women in foster care report having had at least one pregnancy by age nineteen and nearly three quarters report one or more pregnancy by age twenty-one.[14]

The problem of preparing aging-out youth for "independence," the termination of state assistance, is one of the most pressing concerns of the state, nonprofit, and philanthropic establishment administering the foster care system. It is in this area that the rhetoric about "breaking the cycle" achieves the most urgency, as each adolescent remaining in care has an expiration date looming over him or her.

Until 1991, federal funds could not be used to benefit any child beyond age eighteen, but that year Congress allowed states to provide "after-care" services and create the option of allowing a foster youth who is enrolled in school or employed to remain in foster care until age twenty-one. All states are mandated to continue Medicaid eligibility to age twenty-one. The grim statistics cited above indicate that these modest provisions have not been effective in supporting very many youth during the "transition to adulthood" process.

Motivated by an understandable desire to prepare young people for the moment they are cut loose by the state that has taken responsibility for raising them, professionals within the system increasingly regiment the transition process. Various models for imparting "life skills" such as time management, budgeting, interview behavior, and so on, are implemented, studied, and continually revised. Programs aggressively market the idea that college attendance will lead to enhanced earning power, often on the basis of misleading national averages, and march youth in lockstep toward college. The system has a poor record of facilitating success in college, however. According to the American Bar Association's Center for Foster Care and Education, more than 80 percent of seventeen- and eighteen-year-old foster youth report a desire to attend college, but only 20 percent actually enroll, and between 2 and 9 percent graduate with a four-year degree.[15] Success is often measured by enrollment, and not by completion, and the high percentage of students who drop out after incurring student loan debt is rarely tracked.

Agencies celebrate the heroic success stories of those young people who have "risen above" their family and community background and achieved academic and economic success. Of course the achievements of extraordinary young people should be recognized and praised, but the message underlying the criteria for success is that civic participation means becoming a desirable employee with consumer power and avoiding the failures of their parents.

The regimented transition process mirrors the high-stakes testing and compliance regime that increasingly dominates public education, but it is clear that the looming deadline for achieving independence introduces an additional threat to conform. It also gives those employed within the system no alternative. Under the current system, it is barely possible to imagine a different way of approaching adulthood other than by focusing on the needs of employers, even as the employment outcomes indicate the system is failing to prepare youth for success in the job market.

LGBTQ Youth

A final issue that should be touched on is the relationship of child welfare to oppression based on sexuality and gender identity. The writer Sherry Wolf makes the point that the social organization made possible under capitalism created room for gay consciousness, but that the need of capitalism to enforce a norm of family life and divide the working class led to the construct of gay identity as a threat to family life.[16]

When Arkansas passed a referendum in 2008 prohibiting gay people from adopting or fostering, it was recognized as a terrible violation of the civil rights of prospective parents. We should also add that it's an assault on many of the children who enter care, particularly adolescents, because the foster care population includes a significant number of LGBTQ (lesbian, gay, bisexual, transgender, and questioning) young people.

The rejection of LGBTQ youth by family, and consequent remand to the care of the state, is common enough that such youth form an identifiable segment of the foster care population. What does it say when the state that assumes parental responsibility defines them legally as second-class citizens? How much harder does it make it to find welcoming homes? The problem isn't just confined to states that codify homophobia in their laws.

Even in New York City, where a recent child welfare commissioner is a married gay man and adoptive parent, the system relies on foster care agencies affiliated with religious institutions that discriminate, and recruiting practices for foster parents often involve such institutions. There is a strong initiative designed to find welcoming homes for youth who already identify as LGBTQ, which is a positive, needed step. Children come into care at different ages and some may identify as LGBTQ at some time in the future. The city takes responsibility for finding them homes, but in doing so may be guaranteeing that some children will experience rejection and oppression from the parents to whom they are handed over.

In the 1980s Catholic foster care agencies in New York City asserted their power by withholding beds—essentially staging a partial shutdown—in order to preserve their right to discriminate against gays in hiring. An artificial crisis was created, and children were warehoused in hospitals, offices, and over-capacity congregate care settings, but the diocese was able to get the city to back away from enforcement of its antidiscrimination laws against publicly funded faith-based foster care agencies.[17]

The presence of many faith-based organizations in the field of child welfare services is troubling. As such organizations push for "religious freedom" exemptions from nondiscrimination statutes, with renewed impetus after the winning of marriage equality nationally, the system might continue to put LGBTQ youth, whether so identified now or in the future, into the care of organizations that find them unworthy of equal treatment.

Transgender youth face distinct challenges in foster care and child welfare institutions, as they do in the larger society. Unfortunately, they are included in the broader category of LGBTQ youth, so there does not seem to be data indicating the extent to which transgender youth are overrepresented in care. However, given that more than half of transgender youth report family rejection, it is likely that there is such overrepresentation. Very few states have specifically addressed gender identity and crafted protections so that youth have the right to assert their gender identity on assignment to congregate care facilities, in how they are addressed within foster homes, and so on.[18] Involvement with child welfare puts transgender youth at risk of placement in facilities where harassment, bullying, and violence may occur. It is important that greater attention be paid to the needs of transgender youth, including protection from harassment and bullying, and that the right to assert their gender identity when in state custody become universal.

ONLY ONE REAL FAMILY*

By Kamaal Dashiem Crumpton

Entering foster care was the worst and angriest experience in my life. I was asleep when a social worker came to the door with several police officers. I heard a knock on the door, but before I could ask who it was, the social worker burst in without my permission. "Grab your things . . . you're coming with us," she said. I was fifteen years old.

"Please don't take him! Please don't take my baby!" my mom kept repeating with tears running down her face. There were two officers holding her back. She was trying to grab me away but her attempts were futile. The social worker was asking me questions but I didn't speak a single word until I got into the car. I have never cursed so much in my life. The social worker seemed like a vulture who wanted to devour me.

We drove to the main Children's Protective Services building in Manhattan. I stayed there for about a week. I thought this was a group home at first. I saw a guy who had a huge scar going across his stomach. I wondered if he got it from being in here. I was glad later on that day I was able to leave even though I wasn't going home.

Ms. Davis

I was only in my first foster home for about a week. I lived in a few other places over the next year. I never got used to any of them, and I always wanted to be back with my parents. Then, at the beginning of my junior year in high school, I moved to Ms. Davis's house. Ms. Davis seemed really nice, a respectable lady who had a job at a junior high school. She looked like she was in her early thirties but said she was much older. The house was nice, with three floors and a back yard. I was only her second foster child; before she'd had a baby girl who stayed there for a few months. She had never accepted teens in her home, so this was something new to her as well. She was friendly and lenient most of the time. When she did bug me, she was fair about it. "Kamaal, before you walk out, clean your room. It'll be easier on the both of us if we cooperate." She asked me to call her

---

* Reprinted with permission from *Represent: The Voice of Youth in Care*, see www.representmag.org.

Auntie Fee-Fee, but I wasn't comfortable doing that. I liked her, but I didn't want to give her any type of family title. The love from my real mom just felt more genuine, even if she was spanking me; the same thing for my aunts. Asking me to call her Auntie seemed like Ms. Davis was asking me to love her. That didn't seem possible to do with someone in the system. No matter how long I stayed with her, I knew where I belonged—with my real family.

Everyone I Cared About

In the middle of that December I met Akeisha. I was sixteen and she was fourteen. We were both into poetry and drama and shared views on movies and actors. She was funny, too. We were attracted to each other's company right away. We started dating, and took it slowly at first. But soon we found it hard to part from each other, and I walked her home every day after school. She lived in the Bronx, which was about two and a half hours away from Ms. Davis's house in Queens, but I didn't care because I just wanted to get to know her more. We would sit in front of her building for hours, holding each other close and talking about our views of the world. Akeisha made me feel as if I needed no other.

Although my curfew was 11 p.m., sometimes I wouldn't get home until three in the morning. Some nights I would crash at Akeisha's house (in a separate room). Ms. Davis asked if I was sleeping at my girlfriend's house and I told her the truth. She was pretty cool about that; she just asked me to call if I wasn't coming home.

Leaving Queens was a wonderful feeling. Being in Queens made me feel isolated. Everyone I cared about was in the Bronx—Akeisha, my friend Daniel, my parents, my five brothers, and my baby sister. I wanted freedom from the system and I felt free when I was with Akeisha.

At this point I was seeing my parents and the rest of my siblings at family meetings every Monday and Wednesday. For the most part the meetings were really fun and heartfelt (except for the caseworker who seemed like a vulture waiting for my parents to mess up). None of us agreed with the reason I went into care—it was something my parents did that I don't want to talk about except to say it had nothing to do with me and didn't harm me. We missed each other and wanted to be together again, and we were all devastated when the court terminated their parental rights.

She Tried

After being with my real family, it was hard to go back to Ms. Davis's, even though she was pretty cool. She did try to keep me happy. She made food that I liked and had video game systems, and for a while I had my own room. But no matter what she did, I couldn't feel at home in her house. Ms. Davis could never be my mom, my aunt, my sister, or any part of the real family I have outside of the system. She would ask me if I wanted my brothers to visit the house, which was nice, but that didn't help me accept her as family. But she kept trying. After I had lived there a year and a half, she asked if I wanted to be adopted. I was furious. She was well aware of how badly I wanted to go back to my parents, yet she still had the audacity to ask me if I wanted her to be my official legal guardian. Just because my parents lost their rights didn't mean I had lost all hope of going back with them. She knew how hard my parents were working to get me back. To be aware of how much my family wanted to be reunited and still ask a question like that felt like a high level of disrespect.

Web of Rebellion

Though she may have meant well, Ms. Davis's request to adopt me only pushed me further away. I wanted to be with Akeisha all the time, and she began to run away from her home as well. She was younger than me, and I didn't want her to endanger her home situation. But I wasn't as strong as I should have been, and I allowed her to get caught in my web of disrespect and rebellion. This got us in the deepest trouble of our lives.

One Saturday afternoon, almost two years into our relationship, I picked Akeisha up at her mom's house. It was a cold fall day, and we headed to her friend's building in the projects nearby. But we never made it to the friend's apartment; instead we got comfortable sitting on some steps in a dark stairwell. The only light was from the signs above the fire doors. We heard heavy footsteps on the floors above and below us. The elevators were going up and down more than seemed normal. Then we heard five or six people coming up the stairs, and suddenly in front of us were a group of police officers in uniform. I told them we were just sitting there, but one replied, "There is a lot of illegal activity going on in these buildings; we have to take you in." Then they walked us out of the building, cuffed our hands behind our backs, and put us in the back of a big police van.

At the station, they asked me if there was someone they could call for me. I didn't have my grandmother's number or my dad's, but I did have Ms. Davis's number, so they called her. Then they put me and Akeisha in cells next to each other and told us not to speak. Ms. Davis didn't come to the station, but she must have said something reassuring, because after four hours they let both of us leave. Akeisha's mom came to pick her up and I took the subway back to Ms. Davis's. She asked, "What were you doing that got you in jail?" She didn't look that worried. It seemed like she was expecting this since I was gone so much. I told her the truth, and she said, "What am I going to do with you?"

Burning Bridges

I didn't answer. I felt bad about the mess I was putting her through. She never did anything I didn't like. She was kind, she was cool to talk to, and she was fun.

"Kamaal, I can't keep doing this with you. Now we are going to have to find some common ground. I'm sure you don't want to burn your bridges with me or anyone else you deal with because you never know where you will end up."

I understood everything that she was saying to me; I just had it planted in my head that I didn't want to see Akeisha any less, and I didn't want to be forced to call anyone just to tell them I was OK.

"So Kamaal, what will it be? It's either you stay and try to work this thing out with me or . . . you do the same thing in another home." I didn't answer her immediately, but I knew that I didn't want to live with her anymore.

Not My Mom

There was nothing wrong with Ms. Davis, but I just didn't want a foster parent. I didn't want a social worker and a caseworker and legal guardians either. I didn't want to travel for more than two hours to Queens to see people that I didn't know or care about. Why should I conform to the rules and regulations of a system that took me away from my family?

I felt somewhat prideful; I felt that I was showing everyone within the agency that I was not afraid to move around. No matter where I was placed, I was going to see the ones I wished to be with the most, whether it was my girlfriend or my family. Leaving Ms. Davis's felt like a step closer to having control over my own life.

But now, two years later, I look back at how I handled Ms. Davis and I see how selfish I was. I was actually putting people who were trying to help me in a bad position because I couldn't compromise. It's not that much to ask that I would call when I was not coming home or coming home late. I just wanted to spend time with someone I was close with and who I chose, unlike Ms. Davis, who was assigned to me. But I realize now that Ms. Davis was actually much better than a lot of foster mothers.

Since leaving Ms. Davis's home, I've taken more responsibility. I live in a foster home where they allow me more time to myself. The same rules apply—call and no AWOLing—but I can live with that now. I realize I owe foster parents some cooperation. If I got put in a sticky situation while in their care, they might not be able to take care of any children anymore. I don't want to put them in that position. But my foster parents, whoever they are, need to know that they can never be my mom and dad. If I had another shot with Ms. Davis I don't think I would take it. I would apologize for everything I did, but living with her again? I really can't see that happening. I don't want any foster mom–foster son bonding. I can follow the rules of a house as long as there isn't any confusion between us about who my real parents are.

MENTALLY ILL, GAY, AND HOMELESS[†]

By Yaselin Serenity Solis

I went into foster care when I was eleven. I went through a lot as a kid and have struggled with my emotions. I've gotten in a lot of trouble, including fighting, and have done impulsive things. From age sixteen to eighteen I lived in a residential treatment facility (RTF) in Harlem called August Aichhorn. Aichhorn was a locked-down psychiatric facility, so I couldn't go out when I wanted to. At the time I didn't like being told what to do, but looking back, the structure helped me learn what I had to do in the real world.

I met with a therapist once a week, and I saw a psychiatrist once a month for medications. My therapist wouldn't let me leave until we spoke about the disturbing things from my childhood. Talking about my feelings helped me because before (and even now sometimes) I would keep my feelings bottled up inside until I couldn't take it anymore. Then any little thing would set me off.

Once I started talking about my feelings I grew less angry. I began to learn why I was so angry and how I could cope with strong emotions. I was able to go off medication. But I'm still impulsive and if someone touches me, I might hit them.

Aichhorn was only for people up to age eighteen. When I turned eighteen, I was moved to Aichhorn's Young Adult Supportive Living program (YASL), six blocks north. It is for people eighteen to twenty-five, charges rent, and is not part of the foster care system, but rather the state mental health care system.

The rent money was taken out of our Social Security Supplemental Security Income (SSI) checks. I receive a total of $796.70 every month because of my mental diagnoses: bipolar, post-traumatic stress disorder (PTSD), and anxiety. It seemed odd to pay rent and still have a curfew. Plus, I felt there was favoritism at YASL. I would get locked out of my apartment for being late, whereas a boy who did the same thing was let in. It made me angry, and I hated living there. I had a therapist there, but

---

[†] Reprinted with permission from *Represent: The Voice of Youth in Care*, see www.representmag.org.

it was hard to start over with a new person, especially since I only saw her once a month.

Missing Curfew

Before I moved from Aichhorn to YASL, about a year ago, I met my girlfriend Izzy. She's twenty-two and has an apartment in a New York/New York III supportive living building. NY/NY III is for people who are chronically homeless, people with mental illnesses, people with HIV/AIDS, and young adults up to twenty-five years old who are leaving or recently left foster care. NY/NY III only allows Izzy to have guests three nights a week. If I were at her apartment more than three nights, it would result in a write-up. Ten write-ups is an automatic eviction. We pushed against that rule, though, and I often stayed there and missed my curfew at YASL.

After I'd been at YASL for a month and a half I told Izzy I wanted to sign myself out. My caseworker did petty, strange things to me: Once she tried to deny me a weekend pass because she said I needed to have my hair done. For one thing, I had gotten it done that week; for another, that's not a rule. But Izzy didn't like my plan. "I told you to stay there till you get your own place. I don't want you to make the same mistakes I did, Yaselin."

Izzy had also lived at YASL and signed herself out, and at one point she was homeless. She didn't want me to go through that. She calls me "Miss Bougie" because I like things to be clean and nice. Izzy didn't think I'd be able to handle the streets.

I signed out of YASL anyway, and then changed my mind and went back. But I still kept missing curfew, maybe because I didn't really want to be there. Three weeks after I came back, I was kicked out. The director of the program called me into his office and asked me to sign a thirty-day eviction notice because I kept missing curfew. He said, "I will not have people who don't want to be here. There are plenty of people who are willing to obey the rules who could have your bed." He continued, "You have thirty days to get your belongings out or they will be given to the Salvation Army as a donation."

Homeless

I wasn't that afraid because I ran the streets when I was younger. But I always had a place to come home to, so I didn't really know what it would be like.

Although I was being discharged from YASL, I was still in foster care. (In New York, foster care goes up to age twenty-one.) However, things have gotten really confusing. When I went into care, my agency was Catholic Guardian Society and Home Bureau, and I had several caseworkers from there. Then, at Aichhorn someone named Dominic became my caseworker. When I got discharged from Aichhorn, they assigned me an "Intensive Case Manager" named Ms. Rosa. She still gives me carfare and helps me with paperwork, going to the doctor, applying for housing, things like that. We get together once a week.

I don't even know if Catholic Guardian is still my foster care agency, and I didn't realize that my being homeless at eighteen was illegal for a foster child until my attorney told me. I tried to help myself by calling the supervisor at Catholic Guardian and informing her that I was homeless, but mostly I got voicemail.

YASL didn't offer to try to find me a place to stay. I went straight from YASL to a friend's house and stayed there, but only for a night because I didn't want to be a burden. In desperation, I became an illegal tenant at Izzy's home. We got caught and she was threatened with eviction.

Subways and Shelters

I'll never forget the first night I slept on a train. It was November and I had no blanket, just my coat to cover myself with. I was scared of being robbed, so I left my debit card with Izzy and kept my cash in my bra. I barely slept. I was cold; I was hungry; and worst of all I had to use the bathroom and there was nowhere to go! After three nights, I realized I couldn't handle this. Then I went to The Door, a drop-in center, and they sent me to an LGBTQ shelter called Sylvia's Place. I thought sleeping on the subway was the worst, but sleeping at Sylvia's came close. I had to sleep in the basement on a thin mattress with dirty sheets. The walls are white, like a hospital, except dirty. Everybody was woken up at 6 a.m., and the clothes donated to the shelter were from prior residents.

After one night at Sylvia's, I went back to Izzys's, then back to The Door. There I got yet another case manager. I've had all these different caseworkers and they don't all have the same information, so I have to keep telling my story over and over. The Door case manager recommended that I go to the Ali Forney Center, which is emergency housing for LGBTQ youth ages sixteen to twenty-four. Two days later, a bed became available, and I took it.

Ali Forney is way better than Sylvia's. It does not look like a shelter; it looks like a regular home. The food is home cooked every night, and I don't have to worry about my bed being taken from me. I have a curfew—9 p.m. Monday through Thursday, and midnight on the weekends. Now that I've slept in worse places, a curfew doesn't seem that bad. Since leaving YASL, I keep my belongings at Izzy's apartment so I don't have to worry about my things going missing. I don't carry much with me except my wallet and my phone. Being homeless makes me want to get my life together. I am filing court papers to change my first name; I feel like my old name is keeping me stuck in the past, and I want to move forward. I have a caseworker at Ali Forney, Adrienne, who is helping me with practical things. I also talk to her about my feelings. I like her so far. We started my housing application for supportive housing at New York/New York III.

Being homeless has made me lose momentum in every part of my life. Five months ago, I enrolled in a GED program that also included an internship. The internship was extremely strict—you could only miss three days a month. I missed seven days because I was focused more on where I was going to sleep than on going to school. I would sleep during the day at Izzy's home till 10 p.m. when I had to leave her apartment. And then, I would wander to a friend's place or start my long night on the train.

After I lost the internship, I got kicked out of the whole program. It really hurt me. So my plan is to try to get back into the school or to enroll in the GED program at a community college near me. I am job hunting, mostly online. I want to work in culinary arts, a field that I love.

It's not right that I became homeless at age eighteen. YASL is specifically for people with mental or emotional problems, who are bound to break rules, especially curfew. I think some of the structure of YASL is good, including having the residents get up in the morning and do chores and productive things like school or volunteer services. But if I ran the program, I would punish kids who broke curfew by taking away their weekend passes or giving them a cut in their allowance. I wouldn't throw them out when they have nowhere else to go.

A Future Without a Net
I would also make emergency and supportive housing for youth in crisis look inviting, instead of dull and scary like at Sylvia's Place. Ali Forney looks like a home because the walls are painted nice colors. The staff made it feel safe and supportive, and my caseworker is helping me move forward.

Izzy and I are engaged now, and I think that if we obey the rules of her apartment that we eventually can get supportive housing for families with mental illness and live together. I hope by the time I turn twenty-six I'll be ready for our own apartment—that I'll have saved up money, hopefully from a job as a chef. I hope to have a solid foundation that would help me from falling back into homelessness.

This experience has made me feel independent in some ways—for example, nobody in my biological family even knows I've become homeless. Caseworkers are helping me, but I still feel alone because they won't be there for me forever. Between ages twenty-one and twenty-six, the safety net gets taken away. I've learned that if I don't make the effort, things won't come to me.

FIVE

Foster Parents

Regulation and Exploitation of Foster Parents

At its inception, the practice of "foster boarding"—the placement of children by the state or by charities to whom the state delegated its authority—was considered mutually beneficial to children and foster parents. Children received the benefit of a wholesome upbringing by substitute parents able to provide, food, clothing, a home, and access to education, while the foster family got household or farm labor at a time when such labor had considerable economic value. As economic, technological, social, and legal change minimized the value of children's labor, the state subsidy for the upkeep of the child became the means by which foster parents recouped the value of the care they provided.

While in practice difficult to adhere to, certification requirements across the country tend to favor economically "stable" households meeting various normative standards. All states require that prospective foster parents provide proof of sufficient income to cover their housing costs and basic expenses without relying on a foster care subsidy (although there are some exceptions for foster care involving hard-to-place children and youth with "special needs" classification). They further require that the foster home meet space and facility requirements that vary from state to state.

In theory, the subsidy merely covers out-of-pocket expense, and foster parents are not interested in being compensated for the value of their labor or in receiving a contribution toward their rent or mortgages. Some of the system's critics—including many in the communities most affected by the child welfare system—deride foster parents who are "only interested in the check." The criticism is fueled in part by highly publicized cases of abuse. In one case profiled on a national news program, Jacqueline Lynch, a foster parent in Florida took in a large number of children with special needs (eligible for a higher foster care rate), and proceeded to abuse and neglect them for a seven-year period ending with her arrest in 1997. While she collected approximately $150,000 annually in payments, the state ignored the children in her care, failing to visit for roughly two years.[1] Such extraordinary cases of abuse and failure of oversight provoke justifiable outrage, but they obscure a number of issues that deserve reasonable consideration.

To prevent the kind of abuse and exploitation found in the Lynch case, local social service departments vet prospective foster parents to ensure they have adequate financial resources. At the same time, pressure to keep enough homes to ensure children do not linger in institutional reception centers or congregate care means there is a tremendous incentive to get foster parents certified. After placement, caseworkers conduct home inspections, collect receipts, and administer special allowances for clothing, back-to-school supplies, and so on. Case records are in turn audited to ensure that the required oversight is occurring. Caseworkers and those involved in certifying and monitoring foster parents receive a salary for their work. They are not, however, routinely accused of exploiting children for financial gain.

In 2008, the CEO of the Children's Aid Society in New York, who runs the organization founded by Charles Loring Brace, earned a base salary of $407,252, with total compensation including bonuses, deferred compensation, and nontaxable benefits of $676,424. CEO salaries at other foster care agencies in New York City are nearly as generous. The median compensation for CEOs of twenty-seven of the city's foster care agencies reviewed by the author was $251,062, with the lowest being $139,120.[2] High-ranking officials with public child welfare agencies commonly retire or resign to accept executive positions within the nonprofit foster care establishment, allowing them to cap off their careers in the service of children with a high salary and generous benefits.

We should not conclude on that basis that they lack dedication or passion for the work they do or the children they serve. We should, however, question a system that polices the actual caregivers to make sure they are not benefiting in any financial way from the care they are providing, while generously compensating the executives, lawyers, and public administrators running the system. Caseworkers and other employees working under the managers are also paid, although in their case it's likely to be barely a living wage.

The ideology of the system holds that the work that parents do cannot be compensated without destroying the substitute-family relationship the system seeks to create. If they are paid, the logic goes, they will be more like professional caregivers than parents. These relationships are, however, commonly subjected to intrusive oversight, supervision, and regulation of activity, features more consistent with employment than parenthood.[3]

Much of the oversight is necessitated by the fact that everyone involved in the system knows that many foster parents are in reality dependent on the subsidy. Foster children come from poor families living in poor neighborhoods, and in most jurisdictions foster parents are usually recruited from these same neighborhoods. There is a private adoption industry catering to middle-class and affluent families, but few of these families would tolerate the demands and supervision imposed on foster parents.

For years, the system has had the stated goal of preserving family ties and reducing the trauma of foster care placement by recruiting relatives to serve as "kinship" foster parents. Another goal is to find placements geographically close to the child's family and home community. These goals make it even more likely that a child will be placed in a low-income household, perhaps only marginally better off financially than the one from which the child was removed.

Knowing that, of necessity, all the money coming into the home will be needed to cover the cost of housing, utilities, and food, the system nevertheless maintains the pretense that the subsidy can be segregated and administered for the sole benefit of one member of the household. The result may be tension and distrust between the caregiver and those responsible for monitoring her, although many foster parents and caseworkers forge effective, supportive working relationships.

Foster parents are overwhelmingly working class, and the need to comply with various obligations—including bringing the child to family visits and appointments scheduled by caseworkers—limits their ability to earn money outside the home. A study of households containing one or more unrelated foster children found that nationwide, the mean household income in 2006 was 24 percent lower than the mean household income for households containing children generally. Some 15 percent of households containing foster children were subsisting on less than $20,000, and nearly half were paying more than 30 percent of household income for housing cost (compared with a little over a third of households containing children generally). The same study cited evidence that households in which children are placed in kinship foster care are even less well off, and are twice as likely to be classified as low income.[4]

The idea that a foster parent is exploitive if she seeks to stretch subsidies to help cover the rent and other household expenses ignores the tradeoff of care for labor embedded in the origin of the system. It also betrays a bias in favor of families economically secure enough to pay for adequate space to house foster children without any contribution to rent and other basic household expenses, as if such economic security correlates to better parenting.

Foster parent recruitment also displays hostility to the poor and to people of color in the manner in which criminal history is screened. Background checks are necessary to ensure that the state is not placing children with people whose habits or propensities will pose a danger, but there are arbitrary and discriminatory rules about how criminal convictions are assessed. In Alaska, for example, any offense involving a controlled substance will automatically bar the convicted person from being certified for ten years. But drunk driving will trigger the ban only on the third offense. Some crimes with a direct bearing on responsibility for children, such as contributing to the delinquency of a minor or custodial interference, result in only a five-year ban. Thus, a misdemeanor marijuana possession arrest would bar an individual from becoming a foster parent for ten years, while an act directly jeopardizing a young person might bar an applicant for half as long. Since people of color, although no more likely to use marijuana than whites, are far more likely than whites to be arrested and convicted, the hierarchy of offenses triggering a ban will have a discriminatory effect.

Foster parent qualification standards enforce other norms not directly related to the ability to care for children. Seven states have requirements that any couple wishing to foster must be legally married. Virginia requires that foster parents have either a bachelor's degree or a high school diploma/GED and one year of experience in childcare. Virginia further requires that not just the foster parent but any adult who assists in caring for the child or children be able to speak and read English.

Some Foster Parents Are More Equal Than Others

Foster parents are by no means equal in influence. In many states, fostering and adopting has become a form of domestic missionary activity for fundamentalist Christians. Harkening back to the Orphan Trains, these foster parents seek to inculcate children with certain values specific to their own movement. One foster parent runs a blog entitled *Raising Servants of Christ* where she describes her activities as a parent and foster parent. Among the children she and her husband foster are two siblings of color identified by the nicknames given them by the foster family, "Coconut" and "Cocoa Bean," and a white child nicknamed "Blue Eyes." The blogger writes: "This blog is about being Servants of Christ. We strive to be good servants every day by taking back our kids (and ourselves) from the world, homeschooling, living frugally on one income, and the joys and heartbreaks of foster care."[5]

While the religious motivation is certainly primary, it's noteworthy that in this case the mission coincides with the interest in "living frugally on one income" so that the mother can stay home to homeschool her birth and adopted children. As she describes in the blog, they receive foster care and adoption subsidies, calculated at the higher rate for "special needs children."

In some states, foster parents are permitted to homeschool foster children if the birth parent doesn't object. Other states allow it if the public agency gives permission, as in South Carolina, where the statute makes no mention of the child's birth parent.[6] States that permit homeschooling of foster children tend to be those in which Christian homeschooling exercises political power.

Adoption as a missionary activity attracted scrutiny to the phenomenon of "rehoming," where adoptive parents disappointed with the children they have adopted seek to place the children they have adopted with different families. Rehoming has occurred with religiously motivated domestic adoption, although the practice is most common with international adoption. It exists in a legal gray area, but is basically unregulated once the original adoption is finalized. Websites and online forums exist for adoptive parents looking to give unwanted children away, similar to rehoming sites for pets.[7]

The practice attracted national attention after Justin Harris, a member of the Arkansas state legislature, and his wife, Marsha, adopted sisters ages three and six through the state's Department of Human Services (DHS). Tiring of the children after six months, they "rehomed" them with a "youth pastor" who was briefly employed at the Christian preschool owned by the Harrises. About five months later, the man was arrested for raping the six-year old.[8] Explaining the decision to rehome, the Harrises blamed DHS and the children for failed adoption and the "severe injustice" done to them, and blamed the newspaper that broke the story for "smearing" them. Justin and Marsha Harris faced no criminal charges, and Justin Harris continued to chair the Arkansas state assembly committee with jurisdiction for children and youth.[9]

The privileging of locally powerful religious groups extends beyond these states, however. In New York City's foster care system, faith-based organizations have long dominated, and the biggest and best funded have been Catholic and Jewish organizations originally organized as private charities but now dependent on public funds. Until the 1980s, these organizations were permitted to discriminate in favor of children of their faith. Black children, who were overwhelmingly Protestant, were either relegated to poorly funded Protestant agencies or were given lower quality placements by the Catholic and Jewish agencies. In 1972, a class action lawsuit, *Wilder v. Bernstein*, was filed by the Legal Aid Society to force the foster care agencies to stop discriminating. The city attempted to settle with Legal Aid in 1983, but the agencies continued to fight it for five more years. In the meantime, of course, white Catholic and Jewish children nearly vanished from the system, and Black Protestant children became more and more overrepresented. By the time the litigation ended, discrimination was no longer viable for the foster care agencies, as they would have vanished from the market if they did not become nonsectarian in their placement practices and recruitment of foster parents.

SIX

Juvenile "Justice"

"A Kind and Just Parent"

Foster care and programs for "delinquent youth" are considered separate functions of government, often carried out by different agencies or different arms of the same agency. There are a number of similarities, however. Both emerged in their modern form during the same basic period of progressive reform. Both have roots in the bourgeois desire to repair an underclass that is potentially disruptive. Both have gone through a process of increasing racialization during the same time frame.

Programs for youthful offenders began to emerge in the United States with industrialization. Initially, children and youth were locked up for a variety of reasons, and there wasn't necessarily an effort to differentiate criminal conduct from homelessness, vagrancy, begging, or having been abused or abandoned. New York opened its "House of Refuge" in 1825, and it eventually housed more than a thousand children at a time. Similar facilities were built in other cities.

As the nineteenth century wore on, detention for children who became public charges simply because no one could support them fell out of favor. For criminal conduct, courts and legislatures increasingly recognized an "infancy defense," holding that very young children could not form the "guilty intent" to be held responsible for their conduct. While detention occurred, sometimes children initially detained were turned over to charities supported by the wealthy and middle classes for rehabilitation through adoption into a more wholesome environment. In some places, young offenders were sent to rural youth camps. Just as with the Orphan Trains, the assumption seemed to be that a break with the corrupt influence of the urban environment teeming with immigrants would make young people healthy, vigorous, and morally upright.

Despite the infancy defense and early reform initiatives, imprisonment of young offenders with adults continued, especially in large cities. In Chicago, for example, children younger than fourteen were housed in adult jails, and one middle-class reformer expressed her horror at seeing "quite small boys confined in the same cells with murderers, anarchists, and hardened criminals."[1] The comment reveals that mingled with the no doubt sincere concern for the safety and well-being of the boys was a fear of "contamination" by dangerous political doctrines.

Illinois established the first juvenile court in the nation in 1899, handling abuse, neglect, and delinquency. The creation of a children's court came at the same time as the emerging field of psychology began to express the developmental theory of adolescence as a period of rebellion. The progressive vision for the court was to serve as a "kind and just parent" to help young offenders find their way to adulthood. In a variation, two early sociologists said the state should be "a sorrowing parent . . . no longer a power demanding vindication or reparation."[2]

Despite the rhetoric, juvenile court never lived up to the ambitions of the middle-class Progressive reformers. They were underfunded, and tended to be staffed by patronage appointments. Because their mission was ostensibly about rehabilitation and nurturing rather than punishment, the niceties of due process—right to counsel, proof of guilt—were largely dispensed with. In practice, the facilities in which youth were detained represented less of a break with the adult penal institutions than the reformers had promised.

The courts also met resistance from parents and immigrant communities, who suspected the juvenile courts were intended to remove their children to be raised as "proper Americans." In one case, a mob took over the Chicago Juvenile Court and briefly held its first judge prisoner.

Following World War II, greatly exaggerated media reports about increasing youth crime led to a wave of concern about juvenile delinquency. Televised Senate hearings were held in 1955, and J. Edgar Hoover warned of a "flood tide" of youth violence. A counternarrative about young predatory thugs who needed to be held accountable for their actions became more prevalent than discussion of the juvenile justice system as a "kind and just parent."

In reality, youth crime hadn't changed that much since the nineteenth century. Boys charged with offenses tended to be accused of some kind of theft, while girls were often taken to court by parents for "running wild," which often meant having sex. Young people could be locked up for "status offenses"—truancy, incorrigibility, smoking, drinking, sexual activity. If anything, the hysteria about youth crime was fueled by Supreme Court decisions that extended some—but not all—due process protections to young people in delinquency proceedings. *In re Gault* (1967) gave youth faced with detention the right to counsel and other basic procedural protections.[3] *In re Winship* (1970) held that a lower standard of proof was not acceptable to convict a child of an offense that would have to be proved beyond a reasonable doubt for an adult. Previously, some juvenile courts were using the lower standard of preponderance of the evidence, the standard used in civil trials.[4]

Getting Tough on (Black) Youth

Gault and *Winship* were followed by two trends during the 1970s and '80s. One involved the closure of detention facilities because of cost and the perception that children should not be locked up for status offenses. The other was a "get tough" attitude toward young offenders charged with criminal acts. Reserving imprisonment for "criminal" rather than simply "rebellious" youth made it much easier to sell the "adult time for adult crimes" message.

The juvenile justice system became increasingly racialized in tandem with the foster care and criminal justice systems. As Black youths became more and more visible in northern cities, more and more Black children and youth found themselves in juvenile court for delinquency proceedings, and that percentage continued to rise as the "get tough" policies became more popular.

As has been the case since the first juvenile court was established, most males in delinquency proceedings are charged with nonviolent theft, although the "war on drugs" has dragged in many young people as well. In 2003, 68 percent of young offenders detained for delinquency were charged with nonviolent property, drug, or public order offenses. Of those charged with crimes against the person, one of the largest cohorts was detained for simple assault, which is likely to mean adolescents fighting.[5] Violence involving firearms has increased, primarily because firearms are more ubiquitous than they were in the early years of the juvenile justice system.

FBI data indicate that violent crimes are committed by Black and white youths at a 3:2 ratio, but Black and white youths are arrested for violent crimes at a 4:1 ratio. In terms of drug offenses, the disparity is horrific. In Baltimore in 1980, five Blacks were arrested for drug possession for every white arrested. Ten years later, the ratio was 100:1.[6] This despite the fact that Black youths are no more likely to be involved in drug activity than white youths. Blacks are more likely to be remanded, more likely to be found guilty, and more likely to serve a custodial sentence. Among those remanded, Black youth are more likely to go to secure detention rather than an unsecure alternative.

During the 1990s, the number of inmates and detainees in adult facilities quadrupled, and then began to fall somewhat, partially as a result of federal legislation limiting the ability of states to put juvenile offenders in adult jails and prisons. The law allows children and youth charged or convicted as adults to be housed in either adult or juvenile facilities. Thus, adjudication as a youthful offender will limit placement options, while a decision to seek conviction as an adult will not.

The most notorious manifestation of the "adult time for adult crimes" movement was Proposition 21 in California, a ballot referendum passed in 2000, which mandated adult prosecution for certain specified offenses and vastly increased penalties for juvenile offenses deemed "gang-related." It passed overwhelmingly on the argument that there was a growing epidemic of youth violence, although violent crime by young offenders was actually dropping at the time.[7]

Imprisonment of youth has declined during the current century, but inconsistently. Between 1997 and 2003, twenty-five states saw a decline in detention rates, while twenty-fives states and the District of Columbia saw an increase.[8] One change has been the emergence of kids' jails as a profit opportunity. About 60 percent of facilities are now private, although they account for less than half of the beds in the system. Although some are run by nonprofit organizations, many are run for profit.

Locking Up Kids for Profit

The jailing of children for profit opens up new possibilities for abuse, as the business plan for a for-profit jail requires a steady stream of detainees. The industry can be expected to engage in lobbying and corruption to maintain cash flow. An extreme example occurred in Luzerne County, Pennsylvania, where two judges were convicted in federal court in 2010 and 2011 of racketeering for accepting nearly $3 million in kickbacks over five years from the operator of a for-profit juvenile detention facility. In return, the judges ensured that the facilities remained filled with kids charged with offenses in delinquency court. As a result, the rate of incarceration for youth found delinquent in Luzerne County was roughly two and a half times the statewide average, and the percentage of youth appearing without an attorney was nearly ten times the percentage for the state.[9]

The Juvenile Law Center in Philadelphia summarized the dynamic that is created by jailing children and youth for profit:

> It is axiomatic that for-profit programs are in the business of making money. While detention centers provide some short-term services to youth, their primary mission is control. At their core, detention centers ensure that a youth will show up at trial and not commit an offense prior to trial. For-profit detention centers make their profit based on a headcount. While public detention

centers will stay in business even if their populations are low, for-profit detention centers cannot afford low populations.[10]

Thus, a privatized system is based on a business model requiring an adequate supply of young people to operate at capacity and maintain cash flow.

Another driver of youth incarceration (and racial disproportionality) is the "zero tolerance" movement in school discipline. School systems actively feed children into the youth jail system, often for infractions that would once have earned a student an in-school punishment. In the Luzerne "Kids for Cash" scandal, the schools were a vital part of the scheme:

> By 2005, school officials were well aware that the one certain way to rid themselves of a troublemaker was to call the police, because this would get the child before [Juvenile Court Judge] Ciavarella. These kids were not only disciplinary headaches, they often were low achievers academically and dragged down test scores, making it doubly desirable to get rid of them. Behaviors that once were matters of in-school discipline—shoving matches, foul language, disrespect to teachers—were elevated to law enforcement issues. . . . In short, Luzerne County educators used Ciavarella as their chief disciplinarian.[11]

In October 2012, the Justice Department filed a lawsuit against the state of Mississippi and various government bodies in the city of Meridian, claiming the Meridian school district developed new policies to call the police and have students arrested for "crimes" such as using profanity, disrespect, and failing to obey a teacher's directions. The courts, probation, and other agencies cooperated by promptly locking up the children without troubling themselves with the niceties of due process and effective legal representation. Every child arrested at the request of the school district was African American.[12]

The consequences for the students in Meridian were identical to those in Luzerne. The only thing that made Luzerne an exceptional case was the payment of bribes to judges. Prior to their exposure, the corrupt judges were pillars of the community, and the local school regularly invited one of them to give stern warnings at school assemblies. The community leaders were not outraged because the judges were locking kids up for often trivial offenses, but because they were accepting bribes to do so.

Conditions of Confinement

Consistent with the notion of the state as a "kind and just parent" concerned with the welfare of the young offender rather than retribution, juvenile detention is supposed to be corrective but not punitive. The reality is that juvenile detention facilities use essentially the same punitive measures as prisons. A 2009 review commissioned by the US Justice Department analyzed 79 of the 110 suicides that occurred in juvenile detention facilities during the four-year period between 1995 and 1999. The study found that half had been in solitary confinement at the time they committed suicide, and 62 percent had a history of solitary confinement.[13] In 2014, the Youth Law Center filed a complaint seeking investigation of use of pepper spray against juvenile inmates in San Diego. What they discovered is that pepper spray is often used in combination with solitary confinement. They also found that the extent of solitary confinement is obscured by how facilities can choose their own definition of the term. If the facility says that "room confinement" for days at a time is not solitary confinement because the juvenile is not placed in a designated solitary confinement cell, it will simply report no use of isolation.[14]

"Crossover Youth"

The links between the child welfare and juvenile justice systems go beyond their common origins and the largely unrealized goals progressive reformers set for these systems. Very often, they are dealing with the same children. The most direct connection is the population of "crossover youth" who move directly from the foster care to the juvenile justice system. Washington State estimated that third of its detained youth were or had been in foster care. Other jurisdictions have found between 9 percent and 29 percent to be crossover youth.[15]

The connection continues into adult prison. According to federal data, approximately a quarter of incarcerated adults were once in foster care.[16] Foster care and juvenile justice function as components of the "school to prison pipeline" feeding mass incarceration. As the Luzerne and Meridian cases show, the schools are often participants as well.

One activist who recognized the connections between the two systems is Sharonne Salaam, the mother of Yusef Salaam, who at fifteen years of age in 1989 was arrested for rape and assault in the widely publicized "Central Park Jogger" case. Yusef was convicted and spent seven years in prison before being exonerated when another person confessed. Neither Yusef nor his four codefendants had any involvement in the crime. While her son was still in prison, even while working to establish his innocence, she formed a group called People United for Children (PUC) to work on behalf of children and youth incarcerated in the New York State juvenile justice system. Before long, she realized that foster care was the source of much of the population in juvenile justice facilities, and PUC began to focus "farther upstream" on preventing kids from entering care.[17] Her concern for young people in detention led Ms. Salaam to look at where they came from, and to connect their entry into foster care with their eventual placement in detention. She concluded that the best way to prevent the harm that resulted from involvement with the juvenile justice system was to reduce the likelihood of entry into foster care.

Dorothy Roberts explored the intersections of the foster care, juvenile justice, and adult incarceration systems, and rooted them in the ideology of free markets:

> Over the last several decades, the United States has embarked on a pervasive form of governance known as neoliberalism that transfers services from the welfare state to the private realm of family and market while promoting the free market conditions conducive to capital accumulation. At the same time that it is dismantling the social safety net, the government has intensified

its coercive interventions in poor communities of color. The neo-liberal regime does not unidimensionally shrink government. It equally depends on the brutal containment of the nation's most disenfranchised groups. The welfare, prison, foster care, and deportation systems have all become increasingly punitive mechanisms for regulating residents of the very neighborhoods most devastated by the evisceration of public resources.[18]

As Roberts suggests, the intersection of foster care and detention is not just a disappointing outcome that occurs because we haven't figured out how to make these systems work as intended. In fact, crossover between these systems demonstrates that there is a unity of purpose. The distinction between punitive intervention—supposedly reserved for "criminals"—and child welfare intervention for families and youth is largely artificial. Both serve the function of closely regulating the same families and communities.

There is urgent need for reforms in juvenile justice, beginning with an end to solitary confinement, incarceration in adult facilities, and incarceration of youth with mental illness, as well as the use of community-based restorative justice measures in place of incarceration of juveniles. Examples of programs that have demonstrated success include a program in Indiana that put young offenders to work repairing damage done as a result of break-ins in their own community, another which has them help restore damaged wetlands in the Florida Everglades to work off restitution paid to their victims, and a program run by the Red Lake Nation Band of Ojibwe, which has tribal elders work with young offenders one to one and develop an individualized plan for restitution. These programs have shown reduced isolation of young offenders, greater satisfaction among victims and members of the community, and heightened self-esteem and skill building among offenders.[19]

Since the juvenile justice system is a bridge between the child welfare system and the adult incarceration system, the fight for these reforms should be linked to the fight to reform child welfare as well as the fight against mass incarceration generally.

SEVEN

Toiling Inside the Bureaucracy

Street-Level Bureaucrats

There are a series of vexed questions surrounding the role of professionals in the modern child welfare system, including the extent to which individuals employed within the system perpetuate its most oppressive, bureaucratic features, whether they can be agents of reform, and their position in relation to the institutions within which they operate, such as public and private agencies, unions, professional organizations, and the courts. The field is dominated by the cultures of two professions—social workers and lawyers. Only a small fraction of people employed within the system are formally licensed within one of these professions, but I would argue that most jobs orient to approaches and features brought into the system by one professional paradigm or the other. I would also argue that social work is far more important, because much of the work of the lawyers is process oriented, to ensure compliance with substantive rights and obligations reflected in good case practice.

Before considering the social work and legal professions separately, it's appropriate to consider how people working within the system are situated relative to the children and families impacted. Michael Lipsky's theory of "street-level bureaucracy" is one useful framework, first formulated in 1969. According to Lipsky, a street-level bureaucrat is a public employee whose work is characterized by the following three conditions:

1. He is called upon to interact constantly with citizens in the regular course of his job.

2. Although he works within a bureaucratic structure, his independence on the job is fairly extensive. One component of this independence is discretion in making decisions; but independence in job performance is not limited to discretion. The attitude and general approach of a street-level bureaucrat toward his client may affect his client significantly. These considerations are broader than the term *discretion* suggests.

3. The potential impact on citizens with whom he deals is fairly extensive.

Street-level bureaucrats also have "non-voluntary clients," and their clients are not "primary reference groups," meaning that the bureaucrats feel accountable to other, more organized, better-resourced interest groups. The tendency is for street-level bureaucrats to develop routines and simplifications to manage their environment and meet the performance expectations imposed on them.[1]

This theory is generally applicable to child welfare workers. Workers, whether investigators, caseworkers, or lawyers, operate with some discretion in forming judgments, albeit with layers of management oversight and final say on decisions, and even greater discretion over the way in which a client is treated. Their work also has an enormous potential impact on their clients. Finally, they are accountable to managers for data-driven outcomes, to judges, to the pressures of media attention, and to countless other "stakeholders" with more influence than the parents and families with whom they work. Because of the pressure of caseloads and paperwork requirements, they are also prone to routinization and simplification to manage the work and meet management expectations. Conscientiousness, empathy, and even professional ethics may not always be trumped by the dynamics of street-level bureaucracy, but there will always be a tension that is seldom resolved solely in the interests of the client.

Two child welfare workers who worked for the Los Angeles County Department of Children and Family Services (DCFS) describe the position of DCFS social workers. They are nominally given professional discretion to be exercised in the best interest of the children and families to whom they are assigned, but operate under constant pressure to act in the best interest of the department. In a memoir about their work experiences, they wrote:

> If CSWs [Certified Social Workers] could speak frankly without fear of retribution, many of these well-meaning workers who should place the welfare of their case children and/or families above all else do not feel able to do so. If they felt free to speak the truth, they would say that they are being made to do whatever they're told without question or hesitation, and if they do otherwise, they would find themselves under threat of discipline. They are fully aware that to resist certain morally questionable directives may mean putting any hopes of advancement or even their entire careers in jeopardy. They realize that in demonstrating reluctance to go along with these directives, they may even run the risk of facing trumped-up charges on grounds of insubordination.[2]

Radical and Reform Traditions in Social Work

The modern social work profession has roots in the attitudes of charitable giving and relief efforts by the upper and upper-middle classes. Sometimes the motivation was religious and altruistic. Sometimes it was based on a desire to build bridges between classes and promote an ideal of citizenship. Sometimes, as with Charles Loring Brace and the Orphan Trains, it was fear of disruption. Often, it was probably a combination of all these. As industrialization changed the scale and scope of need by disrupting pre-industrial economic relationships, it became necessary to organize charity. Just as industrialization was rationalizing production in the late nineteenth century to yield more scientific processes and maximize return on capital, there was a similar initiative to promote "scientific charity." In the words of historian Walter I. Trattner,

"Scientific charity, in its attempt to organize the philanthropic resources of the community and to relieve suffering in as efficient and economic manner as possible, was similar to the monopolization and trustification of big business."[3] Scientific charity took organizational form in the local Charity Organizing Society (COS), beginning in the late 1870s and drawing on the large-scale organized efforts to assist disabled Civil War veterans and freed slaves.

"Scientific charity" was never about maximizing resources for the poor; it was about maximizing desired outcomes for the givers in terms of impact on the behavior of the recipients. A local COS, acting through middle- and upper-class volunteer "friendly visitors," would investigate claims of need, and pass judgment on whether the claimants were worthy of assistance. The idea was to stigmatize assistance to encourage self-reliance, and when giving assistance, to limit the quantity and duration to the bare minimum. Trattner summarized the underlying ideology:

> The charity organization philosophy rested upon a series of preconceived moral judgements and presuppositions about the poor, which were embodied in the "self-help" cult of the Gilded Age. Leaders of the movement believed in the individual-moral concept of poverty; they accepted the prevailing economic and sociological philosophy that attributed poverty and distress to personal defects and evil acts—sinfulness, failure in the struggle for survival, excessive relief-giving, and so on . . . scientific charity was based upon a rather pessimistic view of human nature, at least the poor's—the notion that no members of the lower class would exert themselves if they felt secure.[4]

The training COS "experts" provided to friendly visitors evolved into professional social work education, and the attitude expressed is conveyed in the writings of Mary Richmond, one of the pioneers of the profession and developers of the principles of "casework": "In all questions concerning the welfare of children, involving as they do a knowledge of recent and vital changes in city life, a knowledge of child psychology, and a knowledge also of the foundations of the family and of the effects of charitable action thereon, we find ourselves in a field requiring more than any other, perhaps, trained sympathy and clear judgement."[5]

In Richmond's work, there was no sense of agency—or even intelligence—of the poor. It is for "child-saving experts" to deliver advice to parents. To Richmond, the friendly visitor with "trained sympathy" possessed a knowledge of the environment and lives of the poor that was superior to poor people's own. She talked about the transition from the "village ideal" to a time of urbanization and large-scale wage labor, when charitable funds became "veritable engines of destruction to the poor" by interfering with market forces.[6] The answer is for well-trained visitors to apply aid scientifically, protecting the working class from its own corruptible nature.

The settlement house movement, which emerged in the 1880s, competed with the scientific charity approach. Settlement house workers, while derived from the educated middle class, were more than friendly visitors. They lived with and studied the poor, and focused more on improving the living conditions in city slums than on improving the poor themselves. In contrast to the casework approach, they organized campaigns to improve tenement housing, regulate hours, wages, and working conditions, prohibit child labor and provide more resources for public education. Many engaged directly in union organizing, while many more provided support to labor struggles. Some in the settlement house movement attempted to confront the racism experienced by Black residents of the cities. That they were more radical by far than those espousing the scientific charity approach is evidenced by the fact that some settlement house organizations opposed World War I and became targets of the postwar Red Scare. In that sense, the settlement house movement represented a major advance on scientific charity, and marked the beginning of a radical tradition in social work.

Settlement house workers ultimately sought to bridge the gap between the classes by engaging in advocacy to improve the material conditions of impoverished urban workers. The University Settlement House in New York stated that one of its purposes was to "bring men and women of education into closer relations with the laboring classes for their mutual benefit."[7] Thus, while they introduced radical reform politics into social work and developed a more respectful, collaborative approach now dominant in the profession in the form of "strength-based practice," there was a limit to the radicalism of the settlement house workers' approach. They showed a commitment to reducing inequality while defusing tensions between classes, but not necessarily to challenging the fundamental class nature of society.

The backlash against radicalism in social work took the form of an increased emphasis on professional status and training. The onset of the Great Depression brought a renewal of radicalism in social work in the "Rank-and-File" movement, perhaps the high point of social work radicalism and activism. Responding to the collapse of the economy and the desperate poverty of the unemployed working class, many social workers quickly radicalized. Acting initially through radical discussion groups and later through campaigns, public sector organizing drives, and alliances with a range of radical parties and organizations, social workers agitated for militant action against corrupt, punitive local relief programs, for comprehensive social welfare programs and other massive reforms. Rank-and-File was never a single organization, but it was a name adopted by the discussion groups, professional associations, and public sector unions for collaborative efforts. One leader of social work radicalism, Mary van Kleek, proposed transforming social work research into a tool for "rational and social control of industry for the common welfare." While the New Deal measures that were enacted didn't go nearly as far as the Rank-and-File demands, the movement contributed to the climate that made these reforms possible. Active participants in Rank-and-File included Communist Party members and sympathizers, and they followed the Popular Front line and aligned with mainstream liberal reform and professional organizations. During World War II, they largely subsumed their activity into support for the war effort.[8]

The onset of the Cold War led to a new, more powerful spate of redbaiting directed against the most radical currents in the social work profession. Anticommunist purges decimated unions and locals, with the most notable casualty being the United Office and

Professional Workers of America (UOPWA) and the United Public Workers of America (UPWA), both of which were expelled from the Congress of Industrial Organizations in 1950 for following the "Communist Party line." In New York City, UPWA was quickly destroyed by a public welfare commissioner recruited specifically to eliminate communist influence in the unions.[9] Professors of social work were hounded out of universities, hauled before the House Un-American Affairs Committee and its local counterparts, and prosecuted for contempt. Local social welfare departments, universities, and nongovernmental organizations cooperated with investigations into the political views of employees. McCarthyism directed against the social work profession was successful in purging some radicals, intimidating others, and cowing the mainstream establishment, which shied away from reform policy work in favor of professionalization efforts.

The next wave of radicalism came in the 1960s, mostly among younger workers, including both licensed social workers and "nonprofessional" categories of social welfare workers. In union activism, this generation of radicals favored alliance with welfare recipients and collective bargaining demands for better welfare benefits and less punitive policies, in contrast to workers who wanted the union to focus on collective bargaining for "bread-and-butter issues" affecting only the workers themselves. Between 1965 and 1967 in New York City, workers who wanted to broaden the scope of bargaining were able to lead a series of walkouts and job actions with union support. Among the issues they wanted included in the contract were increased benefits and clothing allowances for recipients, as well as lower caseloads for workers. The contract was eventually settled in mediation, where "outside" issues were quietly shelved.[10] Although they were not ultimately successful, their ability to pull the union along with these social justice demands for an extended period represents a degree of militancy for municipal social welfare workers not achieved since, unsurprising in light of the relentless assault on organized labor in the intervening years.

One thing that distinguished this wave of radicalism was its critique of the profession itself. One of the main organizational manifestations was the Social Welfare Workers Movement (SWWM), which formed in alliance with the National Welfare Rights Organization (NWRO), which comprised mainly Black mothers who were or had been recipients of AFDC, after NWRO staged a controversial and confrontational protest at a national social work convention.

One of SWWM's signature positions was a demand for "deprofessionalization," as it maintained that "meaningless professionalization mystified the work, promoted social control, divided the workforce, and alienated the subjects of programs. Referring to the master of social work degree that is the basic credential of a professional social work, SWWM adopted as one of its slogans, "MSW = Maintaining Social Wrongs." SWWM and other formal and informal groupings were most active in support for the NWRO effort to guarantee a right to decent support for families and children.

The National Association of Black Social Workers (NABSW) also formed during the 1960s surge of radicalism and took positions on racial justice and racism in the social welfare field that represented a challenge to the existing professional organizations. As has been noted, NABSW took a position on transracial adoption that sparked ongoing controversy and legislative response. NABSW also took a position against licensure, which it maintained helped to preserve white privilege and hierarchy within the profession, a stance that was at odds with mainstream organizations like the National Association of Social Workers (NASW).

Some organizations, like the Radical Association of Social Service Workers (RASSW), which operated in New York in the 1970s and early 1980s, were critical of NASW for failing to confront the basic cause of the retrenchment in social welfare that began in the '70s. RASSW fought locally against the savage cuts following the fiscal crisis imposed on New York City by the banks and the state and federal governments, recognizing that the fiscal crisis represented an attempt to restore profits at the expense of workers and consumers, especially people of color in the cities. It charged that professional organizations like NASW adhered to "a limited, individualistic approach" coupled with "amiable do-goodism," without an understanding of social and economic forces underlying the backlash.

Limiting itself to ideological arguments, NASW could never be more than an ineffective advocate of liberal reforms. RASSW, however, struggled to define itself coherently. Its activism was intensely local, and did not engage an audience outside the city. Its positions on national and international issues—in favor of full employment and progressive taxation, against apartheid and US aggression in Central America, and so on—did not differ markedly from NASW or the liberal wing of the Democratic Party.

Specialization within social welfare and organizing among distinct populations, including gays and lesbians, and survivors of sexual and domestic violence, meant that while social work activism thrived in the 1970s and 1980s, much of it was disconnected from other efforts. Social work radicals were effective in pushing professional organizations like NASW to take positions on nuclear disarmament, the death penalty, US imperialism in Central America, South African apartheid, and countless other issues that became part of the liberal mainstream within the field.

Radical social work theory also continued to develop as the neoliberal right gained ascendency. One early, influential contribution was *Radical Social Work*, edited by Ray Bailey and Mike Brake and published in 1976. The preface was an essay by Frances Fox Piven and Richard Cloward called "Notes Toward a Radical Social Work." Piven and Cloward proposed four tenets for radical education in social work, although they can also be thought of as counter-tenets to the then-existing foundations of social work education and practice:

1. First, we have to break with the professional doctrine that the institutions in which social workers are employed have benign motives. . . . We must break with such beliefs as matters of doctrine, taking nothing for granted, and, using our common sense and humanity, look at what agencies actually do.

2. Once freed from a belief in the benign character of the social agencies, we can free ourselves from a second item of doctrine that follows logically enough—that what is good for

the agency is good for the client, that the interests of the agency and the interests of the client are basically identical. . . . [T]here is often a profound conflict of interest between the welfare of the agencies and the welfare of clients. But it is a fundamental object of professional education to deny this conflict, to teach students that the agencies of the welfare state are their agencies. . . . We are, quite simply, being taught to identify with prisons and asylums, with the welfare departments and the urban renewal authorities, and we therefore develop a "learned incapacity" to perceive our own interests or those of our clients. It is a remarkable achievement, reminiscent of the era of industrial paternalism and company unionism, when many workers were induced to identify with their employers. But assembly line workers have since learned that General Motors is not "their" company. We have yet to learn that lesson.

3. Third, we have to break with the professional doctrine that ascribes virtually all of the problems that clients experience to defects in personality development and family relationships. . . . It is an ideology that directs clients to blame themselves for their travails rather than the economic and social institutions that produce many of them. . . . If many professors and employers encourage us to ignore the ways in which various socioeconomic forces contribute to the personal and family problems of our clients, it is for the obvious reason that clients might them become obstreperous or defiant—that is, they might become a serious cause of embarrassment to the bureaucracies. . . . [O]nce we break with this third tenet of professional doctrine, we will become aware, and be able to help clients to become aware, of the multiple links between economic problems and the problems defined as pathology.

4. Fourth and finally. . . we ought to become aware of the ways that "professional knowledge and technique" are used to legitimate our bureaucratic power over people. . . . The

doctrine that "we know best" must be exorcised; there is simply no basis for the belief that we who have . . . university credentials are better able to discern our clients' problems than they are, and better able to decide how to deal with these problems. . . . None of this would be so important were it simply that we did not know very much. But thinking we know a great deal, we often ignore what clients say they need. Even worse, we invoke this witches' brew of "professional knowledge and technique" to brand people with horrendous psychiatric labels, and impose on them the loss of efficacy and self-esteem that inevitably follows. The ultimate absurdity occurs when we persist in stigmatizing people even when our own "diagnostic techniques" fail to disclose evidence of pathology.[11]

Radical Social Work had a significant impact on many in social work education and practice, and Piven and Cloward's tenets are widely reflected in practice and ethical considerations, even if the roots in a radical conception of social work are forgotten. Nevertheless, the systemic pressures imposed on practitioners make it difficult to identify with individuals subject to the power of institutions and systems rather than the institutions and systems themselves. A renewed radical social work tradition would not simply be about liberating the individuals professionals work with, it would also be about relieving the oppression of workers within the system.

Retreat from Radicalism

The neoliberal assault of the 1980s and 1990s had a devastating effect on radicalism within social work. The decline of the left generally was discouraging, and even the word "radical" was largely replaced with "progressive," indicating a growing lack of confidence. Many social workers felt the need to build an alliance with liberals, and thought overt "radicalism" would be a barrier to such possibilities as a broad coordinated fight against austerity. The word was not as important as its confused meaning, as it came to describe anything left of center. The radical Catalyst Collective had published a journal called *Catalyst: A Socialist Journal of the Social Services*. The Catalyst Collective folded in 1987, and its journal ceased publication. In 1990, the journal was brought back under a new name, *Journal of Progressive Human Services (JPHS)*. By 1998, *JPHS* published an editorial lamenting the lack of submissions with radical content, and one former member of RASSW and the Catalyst Collective complained that progressivism had become synonymous with liberalism.[12]

During this period, a focus on working-class solidarity and antiracist struggle had also become fractured by postmodernism and identity politics. This trend had its roots in the process of broadening radicalism in social work to address different forms of oppression, including oppression of women, gays and lesbians, people with disabilities and, of course, people of color. It may have also been a response to the declining influence of revolutionary socialist organizations since the early 1970s, and resentment of the tendency of some socialist groups to formulaic class analysis. Finally, it reflected discouragement and weakness on the left, and a tendency to focus narrowly on language and personal development. The result, however, was splintered areas of activism, many with seemingly radical rhetoric masking a tepid liberal agenda.

Radical teaching and activism did have an impact on NASW, as evidenced by the fact that the organization began to take positions that originated among social work radicals. The NASW publishes a "toolkit" entitled, "Institutional Racism and the Social Work Profession: A Call to Action," which offers encouragement and guidance to social workers on confronting racism in the systems of which they are part, and on changing their employers into antiracist organizations.[13] The New York City chapter sponsors ongoing workshops using the "Undoing Racism" curriculum developed by the People's Institute for Survival and Beyond, and the chapter leadership facilitates an Undoing Racism in Child Welfare work group for practitioners in the field.

On the other hand, NASW has tended to identify itself with the Democratic Party, which presents itself as friendlier to the social safety net than the Republicans. Even when it pursues austerity and dismantles protections for families, it is able to appeal to liberals by promising to fight off even more draconian depredations from the Republicans. The NASW endorsed Bill Clinton's reelection shortly after he signed the Personal Responsibility and Work Opportunity Act of 1996, which eliminated AFDC as an entitlement and which NASW had vehemently opposed. In 2014, on the local level, NASW endorsed Andrew Cuomo's reelection as governor, despite his devastating austerity agenda and brutal assault on public sector unions during his first term. While NASW contributes to advancing progressive practice in the field, its political impact will always be undermined by its loyalty to the Democrats as the lesser evil of the neoliberal parties.

By continuing to support Democrats, NASW—like labor unions—diminishes its power to oppose austerity and advance meaningful reform. Austerity and privatization have been pushed by Democrats for decades, and any power the NASW has to mount sustained opposition is compromised by its periodically corralling its members back into the party at election time to vote for the Democrat because the Republican will do worse. Bill Clinton never had to worry that by pushing a bill that ended AFDC as an entitlement he would prompt social workers to unite with communities for a sustained movement that would survive the bill because of the pullback in its opposition to Clinton once the bill was passed and his reelection campaign had begun. This is the trap liberal organizations fall into when they allow electoral politics tied to the Democratic Party to become the key to their political strategy.

The NASW, to its credit, adopted a Code of Ethics in 1996 containing the following section under the heading, "Social Justice":

Ethical Principle: *Social workers challenge social injustice.*

Social workers pursue social change, particularly with and on behalf of vulnerable and oppressed individuals and groups of people. Social workers' social change efforts are focused primarily on issues of poverty, unemployment, discrimination, and other forms of social injustice. These activities seek to promote sensitivity to and knowledge about oppression and cultural and ethnic diversity. Social workers strive to ensure access to needed information, services, and resources; equality of opportunity; and meaningful participation in decision making for all people.[14]

As an ethical principle and expectation, this is valuable, but the importance NASW places on its relationship with the Democratic Party means that it will never challenge the systems that make effectively challenging "poverty, unemployment, discrimination, and other forms of social injustice" impossible for its members.

Labor Activism in Child Welfare

Radical Social Work, published in 1972, concluded with a manifesto that attacked professionalism and the "pseudo-science" of the case-work method of social work, but that also strongly recommended union activism for social workers:

> We should seek to pressurize the union leadership and fight for official positions ourselves, but our priority is to promote the development of rank-and-file organization through fighting for democratic control by ordinary members at all levels of union organization. We support the trade-union leaders to the extent that they support the struggles of the rank and file, but we must beware of letting the union leaders take the struggle out of our hands and out of our control. To achieve real long-term gains we believe that the creation of a national rank-and-file organization, uniting trade unionists at shop-floor level, is absolutely essential. . . . We must beware of allowing our struggle to become one of passing motions in our union branches. We have to take concrete action to fight for what we believe in.[15]

As noted earlier, the union activism of the Rank-and-File movement of the 1930s was eventually countered by the CIO and government purge of communist union leaders and organizers. Union militancy in New York hit a high point with the strikes and job actions by the Social Services Employees Union between 1965 and 1967, but the city was able to get the contract into mediation where the issues not related to working conditions or wages could be eliminated. Not long after, SSEU became Local 371 of the American Federation of State, County and Municipal Employees (AFSCME), part of District Council 37, the collection of New York City AFSCME locals.

DC 37 was once a powerhouse in city politics, with council president Victor Gotbaum negotiating to bail out the city during the 1975 fiscal crisis by using pension funds to buy city bonds. Far from being a social justice union, however, it was distinctly undemocratic, discouraging rank-and-file militancy and rigging at least one contract vote. In 1997, the union endorsed Republican Rudy Giuliani for reelection. This was a strange endorsement, in particular for Local 371. Giuliani had gutted the city's Child Welfare Administration through attrition, layoffs, and early retirement buyouts, then laterally transferred personnel in from other agencies slated for downsizing. The result was chaos, with child protective workers given massive caseloads and quotas to close cases in order to allow them to open new cases.[16] A highly publicized death resulted from the breakdown in the agency, so Giuliani renamed the agency and brought in a former prosecutor to run it. In the 1990s, DC 37 was plagued by scandals about a rigged vote, corruption, and mismanagement, and this, along with twenty years of antilabor mayors, contributed to its loss of power in the city.[17]

AFSCME is the largest contributor to the Democratic Party, and while it lobbies for liberal legislation and policies, it is closely tied to the party. The other major union in social work and child welfare is the Service Employees International Union (SEIU), which has a similar affiliation to the Democrats. Neither is a union that would welcome—or tolerate—rank-and-file militancy to transform the system in partnership with the families and communities subject to its control.

SEIU was, however, involved in a major strike in the child welfare system that offers at least a glimmer of hope for social justice unionism. In December 2013, social workers employed in the Los Angeles County child welfare system struck for six days, and in February 2014, they won a contact that achieved their demands.

The key demand in the strike was the hiring of nearly six hundred new social workers—a 15 percent increase—to reduce caseloads to levels consistent with child safety. Before and during the strike, the county had said it was ready to hire new staff but refused to commit to a fixed number or time frame, proposing instead a "joint management-labor committee" to study the issue. The new contract has both a hard target and a deadline.

The social workers, represented by Service Employees International Union Local 721, were like other members of the county workforce in having gone without a raise for five years. Local 721 and the county had already come to a tentative agreement on a 6 percent raise over the life of the contract (2 percent per year for three years) for all of the fifty-five thousand county employees represented by the local.

This would provide some relief but was inadequate to make up for the decline in real wages during the previous half decade, when increases in the cost of living were not offset by any increase in earnings. While the thirty-five hundred social workers were prepared to accept the wage package, they could not agree to the settlement without caseload reductions.

The county's "rate of removal," the rate at which children are removed from their families and placed in foster care, is among the highest among major metropolitan areas, with 19.5 removals per 1,000 impoverished children, and 4.3 per 1,000 for all children, compared to 4.6 and 1.1, respectively, for Cook County (Chicago).[18]

Consistent with a national trend, the foster care population in Los Angeles County declined consistently from a peak of more than fifty thousand in 1998. Alone among the largest child welfare systems, Los Angeles saw a reversal of the trend, as the number of children in care dipped to fifteen thousand and then began to grow again.

Critics point to a number of factors, but the most dramatic increases in children being removed from their families followed a series of sensational stories about fatalities from child abuse by the *Los Angeles Times* in 2009, using new legislation opening investigative files from these cases to the media. As the series continued, removals accelerated in what some critics referred to as a "foster care panic."

The stories of children who die as a result of abuse are heart-rendingly tragic, but the *Times*'s treatment of the stories ignored the factors of childhood poverty and societal neglect that contribute to the conditions under which these children lived and died. Instead, the *Times* used the deaths of these children to scapegoat parents living in poverty, front-line child welfare workers, unnamed "bureaucrats," and system change advocates.

The problems with the *Times*'s articles were detailed by a number of critics, whom the *Times* dismissed as "writers who have taken a long-standing position in favor of keeping children out of foster care—even if that means leaving them with abusive parents." Nevertheless, critics catalogued the ways the *Times* misled readers and manipulated data, including inaccurately claiming there was an increase in the rate of deaths as a result of abuse. Most notably, Richard Wexler of the National Coalition for Child Protection Reform documented media-driven foster care panics in other cities, analyzed Los Angeles's data in relation to the *Times* series, and pointed out inaccuracies and questionable practices in the reporting. He described the *Times* series and the official response as "both a failure of political will and of journalistic integrity."

While the *Times* advocated a return to more aggressive removal practices in the name of child safety, it ignored evidence that higher rates of removal do not enhance child safety and may do the opposite, by creating pressure to increase the number of foster beds and burdening oversight mechanisms within the system. Remarkably, the same reporter who had written the 2009 series that resulted in the spike in removals wrote a story in 2013 arguing that the system was putting children at risk when they enter foster care.[19]

One supporter of the 2013 strike, who advocates for parents within the foster care system, stated that the *Times* "really helped to create the conditions that made this strike happen." She said they created the crisis by "throwing the elected officials into a panic."

She said the consequences for parents were increased risk of removal and delays in getting their children back because the system was overloaded. The consequences for children were increased risk of separation, longer stays in care, and a decline in quality because of the pressure to expand the number of homes. For the system's workers, the consequences were higher caseloads, unrelenting pressure to be more aggressive in making removals from administrators fearful of scandal, and inability to properly attend to cases. She added that, even though the strike meant her cases were further delayed, she supported the strikers, and thought most of the parents she worked with did as well.

Strikers set up daily pickets outside the headquarters of the county's Department of Children and Family Services (DCFS). On the second day, Philip Browning, the head of DCFS, made a surprise appearance to plead with the workers to return to work, promising to hire new staff to reduce caseloads. When asked for a specific commitment, Browning said it was a budget issue and went back inside.

Carrying signs saying "Child Safety Now!," about two thousand strikers and supporters rallied outside a county board of supervisors meeting on December 9, the last day of the strike. Seven strikers were arrested for sitting down in the street. The strike was settled with the county's agreement to hire the new workers that evening.

Some strikers adhered to demands that went beyond the caseload reduction formula adopted by the union. Citing a study recommending caseloads capped at fourteen, these strikers supported a demand for fourteen hundred new workers. The county responded that the study predated technological innovations such as iPhones, which it said enabled workers to handle higher caseloads.

Workers demanding these lower caseloads also formulated a series of social justice demands, including closing a tax loophole allowing corporations to evade property tax and a living wage for employees of private contractors doing business with the county. While these positions never became demands of the union, there was clearly some support for social justice unionism among the rank and file.[20]

Lawyers in Child Welfare

The legal profession has less direct contact with families and children but nevertheless has tremendous impact on cases where the state has intervened to place a child in foster care or subject him or her to the control of the juvenile justice system. Lawyers and judges also impact on case practice because of the scrutiny workers are subjected to and because of their power to direct workers. A great deal of time is spent testifying and writing reports for court, and a busy worker is likely to prioritize meeting the expectations of a judge over meeting the expectations of a family with no power over her employer.

Legal advocacy became part of the system to check the power of officials and charitable organizations, which previously made decisions with unfettered discretion. Federal law requires that any state receiving funds under the Child Abuse Prevention and Treatment Act—which is all fifty—appoint a representative for the child. Forty states appoint attorneys, either alone or in conjunction with a non-attorney guardian ad litem, while ten appoint only the non-attorney guardian ad litem.

In 1981, the Supreme Court held that parents do not have a constitutional right to the appointment of an attorney to represent them when the state seeks to place their child in foster care or terminate their parental rights, with the rationale being that their liberty is not at stake—merely their children.[21] Whether they have a right to counsel depends on the statutes of the state in which they live and the willingness of the state to follow the statutes. Some states provide for counsel only when termination of parental rights is being sought, some provide for counsel in other circumstances as well, while some require an attorney in all foster care cases. Only three make no provision at all, but a survey found there were actually eleven states that fail to provide counsel in virtually all cases, so in some states the statutes are not followed. There are also issues of underpayment of parents' attorneys, lack of competence, and excessive caseloads.[22]

As long as the system is based on decisions being made in courts, it is essential that parents have effective representation. The best models provide for "institutional defenders," legal service organizations that provide representation to parents and that include support personnel such as social workers. Los Angeles County has such a model, and New York City has mostly converted its system to an institutional model. Prior to that, lawyers in New York were selected from the "18-B Panel," a roster of private attorneys available to handle these cases and paid by the court at a uniform rate, with their billing subject to court approval. In my experience, these lawyers had little or no support, were often impossible to reach, and were not uniformly diligent or knowledgeable.

While the institutional model is preferable to private attorneys, and private attorneys are preferable to sending a parent into a courtroom to navigate the system on their own, the legal system is an inappropriate place to make decisions about families. The most meaningful communications about cases occur in environments over which clients have no control. Statements made to mandated reporters, child protective investigators, and caseworkers are reformatted and mediated in reports and forms designed by lawyers. To the extent that the voice of the client is heard in court, it is carefully controlled and mediated by the lawyers through direct and cross examination, and the job of the parent's attorney is to advocate for the client, not to assert her right to be heard in her own voice. The experience of unrepresented parents demonstrates this is necessary because of the litigation model we adhere to for decision-making, but providing due process does not change the underlying power structure and give parents agency in solving the problems of their families with the support of the community in which they live.

Impact litigation—class actions or test cases to compel reforms— has been an essential but problematic way of improving the system for families and children. As we saw earlier, in New York, the Wilder case compelled publicly funded faith-based foster care agencies to stop discriminating based on religion, which had an overwhelmingly negative effect on Black children. The litigation took so long that by the time it concluded, agencies saw a declining pool of Catholic and Jewish children, so the demographic changes within the system were at least as important as the class action lawsuit in changing agencies' behavior.

The Nicholson case made it legally impermissible to use the fact that a woman was the victim of domestic violence as the basis for a neglect petition, but as a practical matter she is still vulnerable to be investigated and probed, with a neglect petition being based on other allegations such as "inadequate guardianship." *In re Gault* provided that children had the right to attorneys in the juvenile justice system if threatened with a custodial sentence, but the right is not honored in many states, and even in jurisdictions where it is scrupulously honored kids are incarcerated in large numbers.

One problem with class action litigation is that it empowers the lawyers to negotiate a settlement on behalf of everyone in the class now or in the future. Part of the settlement is that future claims will be barred on the issues that were the subject of the case. Thus, children unborn at the time of the settlement will be bound by its terms, and future efforts at reform will be restrained when circumstances change. So, as important as it has been in addressing key abuses, impact litigation cannot be relied on as the focus of reform.

Most impact litigation is brought by legal service and advocacy organizations in the liberal reform tradition. There is a tradition of radicalism in the law, but it tends to be centered on criminal justice, death penalty work, political prisoners, police misconduct, and so on, or on labor law, environmental defense, civil rights, and civil liberties and other areas. The most prominent organization for lawyers on the American left is the National Lawyers Guild (NLG). The NLG does important work on a variety of issues, but none of its committees, current publications, or most recent conference panels focus on the child welfare system.[23]

Newer-style institutional defenders may represent the best prospect for a different perspective on child welfare in the legal profession. Bronx Defenders, Brooklyn Defenders, and Neighborhood Defenders of Harlem, along with the Center for Family Representation, have been representing indigent parents in New York City since 2007, taking the place of the 18-B Panel, covering every borough in the city except Staten Island. The institutional defenders promote a more egalitarian model of the relationship between the lawyers and social workers assigned to a case, and between the professional team and the parent. All the institutional defenders work together on system change, such as an initiative to pressure the system to develop services for parents with developmental disability. In this effort, they are sharing information and coordinating strategies in order to effect system change, something that was nearly impossible for the panel to do. Significantly, while CFR has the single focus on Family Court representation, the three Defenders offices are part of broader social justice practices that include criminal defense, work against police violence and solitary confinement, and for housing justice. Bronx Defenders expanded the scope of its representation beyond what it is paid to do, providing some advocacy before removal and court filing in the hopes of preventing removals and court involvement. Working with parents at that stage also allows development of greater equality and comradeship between attorneys, advocates, and clients. Finally, Bronx Defenders dedicates at least part of its fundraising capacity to maintaining an emergency fund to provide small grants directly to families to cover emergency expenses and avert crisis.

This model of community-focused, non-bureaucratic legal services office that shows commitment to helping parents solve problems rather than simply protecting their right to due process should be replicated. A change in the model of legal services, rather than just increased funding or expansion of right to counsel, is a demand for reform worth making, especially if it can link struggle within child welfare to broader social justice movements.

OVERWHELMED—HIGH CASELOADS AND PAPERWORK MAKE IT HARDER TO INVEST IN HUMAN CONNECTIONS*

by Anonymous

I took the job of case planner because I wanted to help families, particularly parents.

I believe I have the ability to empathize with people without judging them. I grew up poor in Harlem in the 1980s. My mother received public assistance, and drug trafficking was all around in my neighborhood, so I understand that people can struggle when life is hard.

Before I took the job, I had earned some graduate credits toward a degree in social work. In my job, I tried to practice the social work skills I learned, like empathy and respect. I tried to meet clients where they were. Because of that, I developed a good relationship with many of the parents I worked with. But I found the job very difficult.

Too Many Hours

When I first started, I was told I would have eight to ten cases. Three weeks later I had thirteen. If a case planner quit, or another case came in, the load would increase. Working thirteen cases was overwhelming. Imagine having thirteen kids as a single parent; well, that's how I felt.

I never worked eight-hour days. It was always a minimum ten-hour day without any overtime or comp time. If my schedule was 9 a.m. to 5 p.m., I wouldn't finish work 'til seven and wouldn't get home 'til eight. The time I felt most stressed was when I was asked to help out on a case that started at 5 p.m. and didn't finish until after two in the morning. I had to help a teenager pack up and move out of her foster home because the foster mother didn't want her there anymore. Then I still had to come in the next day for an early morning meeting. It was all too much.

---

* Reprinted with permission from *Rise*, a magazine written by parents affected by the child welfare system: www.risemagazine.org. This story appeared in the Spring 2016 issue of *Rise*.

My child began to tell me that my job took too many hours away from me being with him. About the time I arrived home it was time for him to be in bed or he was already asleep.

Not Set Up for Success

It was also painful for me when parents lacked the resources to care for their children. Once I was trying to assist a parent in reclaiming her teenage children. I could see this mom wanted to be there for them. Still, mom would always say she couldn't attend supervised visits because she was trying to maintain a job to survive, and visits conflicted with her work schedule. I felt poverty was tearing apart the family.

Another mother I worked with had three children, and two of them had different diagnoses. Having two children with special needs was very overwhelming to this mom, and I never felt that she got enough support from the child welfare system or from her children's school. Sometimes I felt like she was being set up for failure.

Documentation, Not Human Connection

Despite the difficulties of the job, the human connection made it worthwhile. When families were open to working with me, when they told me "thank you for your work" and expressed that they liked that I was their worker because I was a support, I felt like I had made their lives better. That, in turn, made me feel like my work wasn't done in vain.

But having so many cases made investing in those relationships harder. Each case had what seemed like a never-ending list of duties. These included meeting court orders, conducting foster home visits, meeting parents at home, assisting parents to find services, assisting youth in any way they needed, monitoring visits, attending court, and on and on.

Sometimes parents really wanted to talk. I wanted to give them my time, so I could show them that the system wasn't just against them, but could also be there for them. But at times I had so much pressure on me that it could be hard to really be present. I'd be listening, but I'd also be thinking about all the other tasks I had to complete. I felt that when it came to my own evaluation, what really mattered would be documentation not human connection. Like everyone else I worked with, I saw case planners terminated, often because of untimely entering of progress notes.

Fear of Termination

That's because paperwork is the legal protection for the agency. If agencies don't have documentation that case planners have done the job the way they're supposed to and something goes very wrong, there can be serious consequences. Supervisors and agencies themselves are under intense pressure.

Still, working with that sense of threat always over my head made me feel expendable and stressed. Because of the overwhelming pressure, I often felt physically ill and down. I would experience intense pressure in my head and the back and sides of my neck. I sometimes thought I might have an aneurism.

Fellow case planners would vent and talk about how overwhelming the job was, and we would also try to assist one another with cases. But providing assistance was challenging because we all had the same stress.

Moments of Humanity

After nine months as a case planner, I found a different position at my agency. Now I have fewer tasks for each case. The biggest difference is that I don't have to go to court. That makes it easier for me to be available to families if they want or need something from me. I feel more successful in helping families feel like the system is not fully against them. That also helps me feel more satisfied with my job.

Recently I ran into a mother in the community who had been able to bring her daughter home, and she gave me a hug. She told me that her child was doing well and she was happy, and it seemed clear from her smile and her warmth that she was genuinely happy to see me. It made me feel good about the work I do.

Not every case planner can simply move to a different role. Many just leave the field. I believe child welfare systems need to understand how important it is for case planners to have manageable caseloads. When case planners and parents have time to build a relationship and time for trust to grow, parents are more likely to stop fighting the system and start working together with it to bring their children home.

EIGHT

The Future of Child Welfare?

A Declining Population in Care

The good news in child welfare in recent years has been the decline in the foster care population. The number of children in foster care declined by 23 percent between 2002 and 2013, from 523,000 to 402,000. The trend is attributable to a decline in the number of entries into the system, and an increase in the number of exits, as well as a reduction of the length of placement in care.[1] Among the strategies cited as contributing to the reduction were improved risk assessment procedures, rapid intervention from preventive services and conferencing with families to address risk factors before removal. These were demands brought to the forefront by reformers aligned with parent organizers.[2]

These are indisputably positive trends, but it does not follow that the system necessarily became better at protecting children by addressing family problems using means less drastic than removal to foster care. It seems more plausible that policy makers chose to direct the system to exercise its discretion to find ways to remove fewer children and employ alternative means of addressing the needs of families.

Interestingly, no decline occurred in the number of children entering care based on allegations of "neglect/inadequate housing." In 1998, nearly 103,000 children entered into care based on such allegations, constituting 40 percent of entries, while in 2008 the comparable figures were 161,000 and 53 percent.[3] This seems to indicate that the system is capable of improving its own practice in avoiding many removals that should not take place, but not of reducing removals caused by poverty and housing instability and homelessness. These problems are beyond the control of the child welfare system. Thus, reform hits a hard limit in terms of its ability to prevent removals.

We should also be concerned about the continuing disparity in removal rates among different jurisdictions. In 2011, rates of removal per one thousand impoverished children in the thirteen largest metropolitan areas ranged from 27.1 in Philadelphia to 4.6 in Chicago (Cook County), with the average being 13.1, a disparity that cannot be accounted for by figures on the incidence of child abuse and neglect.[4] Removal rates vary for political reasons, and this wide variability tells us that the aggressiveness of the child welfare system does not correlate to child safety.

Sometimes, the decrease in removals is attributed to the easing of the "crack cocaine epidemic," just as the surge in the foster care census in the 1980s and early 1990s was blamed on crack. In 1992, independent candidate Ross Perot declared during a presidential debate that babies born to mothers who used crack were "permanently and genetically damaged." President George H. W. Bush and Democratic candidate Bill Clinton hastened to agree that they understood the problem. In reality, while children and families suffered from the criminalization of addiction, no measurable difference in outcomes occurred for children born in poverty to mothers who used crack as compared to children born in poverty to mothers who did not. Poverty, and not cocaine use, was far more relevant in the long run.[5] Removal into care of large numbers of children, and the accompanying eugenic policy measures of coercing mothers into sterilization or implantation with the long-term contraceptive Norplant, were political decisions, not child safety measures.[6] Similarly, the removal of fewer children is the result of a political decision—perhaps driven by fiscal pressure, and not an indication that the system has achieved success or that the lives of children in poverty have significantly changed.

Foster Care Panics

Rates of removal respond to what the National Coalition for Child Protection Reform has called "foster care panics," headline-driven surges created by highly publicized cases of child fatalities. Illinois experienced such a panic following the death of Joseph Wallace, a three-year-old child in the care of his mother. Joseph was "known to the system," meaning there had been prior involvement with child protective services, and this triggered a reaction by media and politicians to blame child protective workers for letting Joseph die on their watch. Within two years, the foster care population in Illinois had surged by 44 percent. Pumping children into foster care caused new safety risks, and while there had been no fatalities of children *in* foster care the year before the panic began, there were five in the following year.[7] Similar panics have occurred in New York City in 1995 and in Florida in 1999.

Interestingly, panics seldom occur when a child dies while in care. There is no corresponding outcry to prevent removals.[8] While it's easy to blame "the system" in such cases (or to lay the blame at the feet of an underpaid, overstretched worker), there is no media or political interest in pushing for a fundamental change. When children die in the care of their parents, however, there is an individual scapegoat, and every parent who comes into contact with the system is seen as having the potential to ruin careers and bring down the wrath of public opinion.

Often, cities modify practices after a panic and reinvigorate family preservation and prevention. Meanwhile, however, families are torn apart and children are traumatized, with either no gain or a net loss in child safety. So while the trend in removals is downward in recent years, any major city is just a week of headlines away from complete upheaval and reorientation toward aggressive removal.

Some jurisdictions have achieved success in avoiding foster care placements by compelling a change in custody within the family without taking the child into care. One such case involved Myls Dobson in New York City, who lived with his mother until 2011, when the city's Administration for Children's Services found she was unable to care for him because of homelessness and mental illness. His father was given custody, but he was later jailed for bank fraud. The father left Myls in the care of his girlfriend, who horrifically abused Myls and caused his death in 2014.[9] Left unanswered is whether housing and effective, readily available mental health services could have prevented his removal from his mother, or why it was necessary to jail his father for a nonviolent property crime when he had custody of his child. The point here is that the strategies employed by the system, whether aggressive removal or alternatives to removal, will not have an impact on child safety unless and until the real risk factors—poverty and institutional racism—are addressed through fundamental change outside the child welfare system. This does not mean that reforms are not important. They certainly are, and grassroots organizing has been a vital part of the positive change that has occurred. There is, however, no way to change the underlying dynamic of the system without fundamental change to the economic and political systems.

Within the field, the emerging trend of reduction in the foster care population was accompanied by promises of "reinvestment" of the considerable savings of money that would otherwise pay for foster care in preventive services—services to address problems through mental health services, case planning assistance, and other supports for families. New York City, which has been the leading edge of the national trend, developed a plan in 2001 to reinvest savings from foster care reduction in a rich menu of services for families, including case management, drug treatment, counseling, benefits advocacy, homemaking services, and other supports. Through 2010, the foster care census in the city had fallen by 58 percent, resulting in some $3 billion in savings. The amount that was actually reinvested in serving families was $380 million, or roughly $1 of every $7.50 saved.[10]

The New York City experience demonstrates two very important things. One is that the inflated foster care population before 2000 resulted from how the system chose to exercise discretion for political reasons. The dramatic drop in the foster care population was not accompanied by a corresponding increase in capacity to serve children at home, yet there was no discernible effect on child safety. It makes sense, therefore, to shift our thinking about the effect of child welfare policy from ensuring child safety by policing families to improving the lives of children and families. Whether aggressive or deliberate, the system does not have the control over child safety that we expect. By and large, families continue to live their lives and struggle with problems without the intervention of the child welfare system. As it is presently constituted—a threatening, punitive, and stigmatizing set of institutions—most families would prefer to avoid involvement. Some actively seek assistance, and there are resource barriers that often prevent them from receiving it. A more adequately funded system that provided assistance readily without the necessity to demonstrate that a crisis point had been reached would not necessarily result in a dramatic decrease in fatalities or serious abuse of children. It would, however, offer relief to children and families on a variety of issues. This shift would also line up with what workers within the system have always wanted its focus to be.

Privatization

A very menacing trend in child welfare, as in education and other functions once thought of as public responsibilities, is privatization. The system has always been privatized to varying degrees in different jurisdictions. As we saw in chapter 2, the model for modern foster care was the Children's Aid Society, a private charity operating largely without governmental oversight. Many charitable organizations, whether secular or religious, became part of the system and remain powerful players. Over time, courts and governmental agencies began to exercise oversight and planning responsibility, with the private entities responsible for placement and services. What has changed in a number of states and cities is the complete privatization of all governmental functions except court review. Since courts typically derive their perception of a case and a parent from reports of caseworkers, this offers little control over a fully privatized system. What is also different is the introduction of a profit motive in states that contract with for-profit providers.

In 1997, Kansas became the first state to privatize its system, awarding contracts to private nonprofit agencies in five regions of the state. Contractors were paid on a per child basis. When it turned out they had underestimated costs and were losing money, the state simply bailed them out with additional payment. The state had little choice, in that it could not legally or politically allow the system to collapse. The bailout of the first statewide privatization experiment, however, demonstrates the difficulty of creating a market for public goods. Since the state remains responsible, it ultimately assumes the risk. Despite noting the difficulties, privatization advocates remain enthusiastic, especially about the potential of a market-based approach to adoption.

Three economists who looked at privatization experiences in Kansas, Michigan, and Illinois proposed a more radical shift to an "auction model" for adoption:

> Economists recommend reliance on markets to allocate goods, services, and resources efficiently. The shortage of white infants and the simultaneous surplus of older, minority, or disabled children is an indication that the adoption system needs reform. Because the goal is to maximize the quality of placement for all children and not use adoption as a vehicle to improve family equity, adoption is a situation where markets can help. Auctions, a special market mechanism, can be used for adoptions in a national market. Auctions will raise revenue for endowing children that are otherwise difficult to place, giving greater numbers of children access to permanent family environments.

Their market would be regulated, of course. They propose a "lemon law" mandating medical testing of the merchandise and disclosure to the potential buyer.

> The high proportion of unhealthy babies drives the healthy babies from the agency in that no prospective parent is willing to incur the risk of getting an unhealthy baby. This phenomenon is

known as the market for lemons and was first used by economists to model the market for used cars.[11]

These passages show where the urge to privatize ultimately leads. Here, the focus is on commodifying children in such a way that an efficient market can be created. If the best way to do that is to emphasize adoption to meet the imbalance between (desirable) white infants and (less desirable) "older, minority, or disabled children," then the system must be "reformed" to meet the needs of the market.

The reality is that privatization has not been shown to reduce costs, and some data indicates that it increases costs of care and introduces new costs related to contract administration.[12] While most privatization ventures nominally exclude for-profit entities, a back door has been found for nominally not-for-profit entities to subcontract with for-profits. One such company is National Mentor, part of a conglomerate with over a billion dollars in revenue, which trades on the New York Stock Exchange. National Mentor has a not-for-profit front, Alliance Human Services, Inc. The company reported in filings with the Securities and Exchange Commission that it uses Alliance to do business with "states and local governments that prefer or choose not to enter into contracts with for-profit corporations." In 2015, a state investigation in Illinois found the company had operated within a "culture of incompetence," and that shoddy operations had jeopardized child safety. The investigators also criticized the relationship between National Mentor and Alliance, which share an office. Alliance seemingly exists simply to sign contracts and act as a conduit to pump money into the for-profit National Mentor. After the investigation went public, National Mentor and Alliance simply pulled up stakes and announced they would no longer do business in Illinois. The state had to take over National Mentor's responsibility for placing 485 children.[13] Presumably, this takeover has considerable costs for the state, and adds further disruption and uncertainty to the lives of the children.

Even when contracts remain in the hands of nonprofits, it is a mistake to think that is a guarantee that funds will always go to services. While one might think that a nonprofit is immune from the profit motive, this is not actually the case. Nonprofits can and do generate revenue in excess of expenses, which appears on their balance sheet not as profit, but as a "change in net assets." What this means is that nonprofit managers can build up the assets of the corporation, with excess revenue being disbursed in executive bonuses, higher salaries, or expense accounts.

Whether the organization is nominally for-profit or not-for-profit, privatization typically creates a class of highly compensated executives, making far in excess of the cost of the public officials who formerly had responsibility for the system. The CEO of All Kids, the contractor for Miami-Dade County in Florida, was paid $182,000 in 2010, rounded up to an even $200,000 with a bonus. Her chief information officer was paid even more, and a total of six executives in the county made six-figure salaries. When Florida's system was public, there was a regional administrator making about half of what the current CEO makes, and a state commissioner who made considerably less than the new, private executive for a single county. Interestingly, these public managers still exist at the same salary levels to provide oversight to the new, even more numerous, and highly paid class of private managers.[14]

Advocates of privatization touted the success of Florida's privatization experience based on the reduction of the number of kids in care, but this was a national trend, occurring in fully public jurisdictions, sometimes—as in New York—to an even greater extent. More telling is the preliminary assessment of the evaluator after Florida's initial four-county privatization pilot was done:

> A particular aspect of three of the four projects that distinguishes them from the traditional approach to the delivery of child welfare services is the present (and planned) use of managed care techniques. *The projects in Districts 4, 8, and 13 are all at risk of financial loss for the provision of services via varying types of capitated payment arrangements, and each is planning to implement some type of utilization review function.*[15] [Emphasis added.]

What the evaluator was saying was that foster care privatization would need to work according to the principles of managed care.

A contractor negotiates a fee per child—the capitation payment. When three of four contractors found the capitation payment sufficient, they planned "utilization review," a managed care euphemism for reducing services to fit within the limits of the payment scheme. With that understanding, Florida moved ahead with privatization.

Other states followed, with similar results. Nebraska attempted privatization in 2009, but was forced to abandon the effort in 2012. Privatization was widely conceded to have failed, and to have created a mess in child welfare that would be costly for the state to clean up.[16] This admission of failure is an exception.

Despite the lack of success, inefficiency, and corruption, the privatization movement has powerful ideological appeal that makes it resistant to evidence of failure. Texas is moving forward with its plan to hand over management of traditional nonprofit foster care placement agencies to for-profit companies. Its first attempt ended in failure, as the for-profit manager handed back the contract after cost overruns and various information technology problems. Nevertheless, Texas remains committed to privatization.[17]

Other risks of privatization include corruption and abuse of the workforce. In Broward County, Florida, workers complained that the chief operating and fiscal officer of ChildNet, the private contract agency, was requiring them to perform work for his private benefit, including searching his BMW for a tracking device he was convinced his wife had placed in the vehicle. This same executive was accused of sexually harassing employees, and multiple executives were accused of disguising personal expenses as operating expenses of the agency. ChildNet was also accused of falsifying data to improve contract performance and housing children in office space.[18]

Privatization is threatening to both workers within the system and to children and families subject to its control. As it has been with education and other "public goods," it can be a strategy to bust public unions and deprofessionalize services by aligning them to a business model rather than an assessment of the best interests and needs of children and families. It can be a means of squeezing services by moving to a managed care model, where the incentive is cost containment. Finally, it commodifies children by placing them in a market. If adoption is the key to profitability, more kids will be funneled onto the adoption track. And, as the Luzerne County privatization of juvenile justice placement described in chapter 7 shows, there is always the possibility of garden-variety corruption to keep the business model on track.

Nebraska's admission that privatization had failed is the exception to the rule. More likely is the Kansas bailout or the Illinois takeover. Elected officials who have staked their legacy on privatization "reform measures" are unlikely to admit failure and very likely to claim unearned success for privatization initiatives.

Families, workers, and advocates within the system will need to unite to defeat privatization, which has considerable financial and ideological appeal to powerful elements in society. Often, however, privatization is proposed when the failures of the public system are most apparent. The fight against privatization should never be about preserving the status quo. It should instead be about an alternative vision of reform, one that changes the relationship between workers in the system and the families with whom they interact. While the bailouts and corruption associated with privatization should be part of the analysis, the argument against privatization needs to unite social justice unionism on the part of public sector employees within the system and assertive advocacy on the part of families and communities.

NINE

Real Reform

Child Welfare, the State, and Civil Society

The child welfare system can call attention to itself in different ways, and this is an indication that it can play different roles. At its most obtrusive, it may appear at a family's door demanding entry, with the threat of returning with armed police if turned away. At its most subtle, it may appear as a poster in a subway car, showing a distraught young woman under the caption, "I never thought he would hurt my child," and exhorting subway riders to exercise caution in choosing caretakers for their children.

The child welfare system has features of what the Italian Marxist Antonio Gramsci called "political society," which he also refers to as the "coercive state." Ultimately, the system is backed by the power to use police to remove children by force and initiate court proceedings to compel compliance or—in the ultimate sanction—terminate the legal parent-child relationship. At the same time, it has features of what Gramsci called "civil society," the network of organizations used to elaborate and disseminate ideology.[1]

Gramsci's "extended theory of the state" holds that civil society maintains "hegemony" of dominant ideas. It thereby achieves consensus accepting those ideas and the consent of those the state seeks to control. Political society, on the other hand, is "the apparatus of state coercive power that 'legally' enforces discipline on those groups who do not 'consent' either actively or passively."[2]

On first reading, the terminology may seem abstract to readers who have never encountered Gramsci before, but I believe there are insights that make it worth the effort to apply Gramsci's framework to the child welfare system. When public campaigns encourage mandated reporters and community members to watch out for children who appear to be poorly dressed or fed, or who may have been left unattended, and to call a hotline triggering an investigation of the parent as a potential harm to her children, the system is reinforcing the idea that the parent is responsible for the situation her children are in. Obviously, when children lack the necessities in life, the community should respond, but it is significant that the means chosen to do so cast the parent as a potential wrongdoer. This idea of parental responsibility for childhood poverty becomes overwhelmingly dominant, or hegemonic, throughout the community and institutions, and even among parents who are investigated. This is the civil society part of Gramsci's theory. For the most part, the community and families consent to the system as it is and accept the underlying assumptions. The power to investigate, compel removal, prosecute parents criminally, apply pressure to obtain compliance with service plans, and ultimately, terminate parental rights, is the coercive part of the theory, and is invoked when consent and compliance is not obtained.

Applying these concepts to the child welfare system as a whole, we see that consent is obtained from whole communities through ideological means, such as public campaigns conflating poverty with neglect and neglect with abuse, training of sentinels in collateral systems, such as schools and health care, classes and support groups for parents who internalize blame for family involvement with the system, and the output of think tanks, foundations, and professional associations that obscure the relationship of capitalism to child maltreatment. The political society, or coercive state, is employed narrowly against those who resist, or when children's circumstances are so dire that coercive intervention has become necessary.

Each is necessary to the other. The elaboration and dissemination of ideology is necessary to legitimize the exercise of coercive power and to obtain the cooperation and collaboration of other institutions of civil society. Coercive power (or the threat of coercive power) is necessary to effect the most intrusive interventions, and to reinforce the reporting mandate.

Establishing a Counternarrative

Gramsci understood the power that the political state has to shape and control the "narrative"—the discussion of issues of importance in society. In what we are considering here, this means presenting in a variety of ways the notion that the biggest threat to poor and working-class children is their parents and not the society in which they live. Gramsci also believed that the working class had the potential to create its own narratives. Again, while Gramsci's thought may seem at first blush to be far removed from struggles within the child welfare system, I believe applying Gramsci's insights and using his terminology is useful in constructing a theoretical framework for such struggle.

Gramsci believed that long before the working class could directly contest the power of the political state, it could engage in the production of different narratives from the ones on offer in civil society. Using Gramsci's terms, this would be "counter-hegemonic ideology" and would help the working class to establish or capture elements of civil society. If this occurs widely throughout the civil state, a "crisis of hegemony" may occur, forcing the state to defend itself by leaning more heavily on coercive power and struggling to reconstruct its ideological hegemony.

Counter-hegemonic narratives can only be articulated, refined, and disseminated through struggles to change the system in the here and now. It can only even begin to challenge the power of the ideology supporting the prevailing system when it is joined with comparable counter-hegemonic efforts in workplaces, schools, and on the streets of cities and towns.

The elements of civil society concerned with child welfare regulation can be among many spaces in which the working class tries to establish counter-hegemony. This will begin by contesting the hegemonic narratives concerning childhood poverty and the problems experienced by poor families.

The conservative narrative leans toward moral failings to be remedied by instilling personal responsibility, while the liberal narrative leans toward individual pathology to be remedied by a treatment model. While much of the mainstream discussion in child welfare tends to be focused on the narrow contested ground between these two approaches, the similarities between the two are more significant than the differences. Both situate responsibility and blame on parents and caregivers, and both ignore institutional racism and economic inequality to varying degrees. The conservative approach denies the role of racism and inequality in child maltreatment, while the liberal approach acknowledges it as a causative factor, but—outside of workers, professional organizations, and think tanks connected to the child welfare system—fails to connect confronting racism and inequality to reform measures and system change in child welfare.

In the case of child welfare issues, a counter-hegemonic ideology would explain that working-class parents are expected to provide all the labor and resources required to raise children who will be the source of labor to benefit the owners of capital. The state, which serves the owners of capital above all, regulates poor and working-class families in such a way as to situate the blame for childhood poverty and deprivation on parents and poor communities rather than on capitalism for creating the conditions for ever-worsening inequality. Such a narrative would assert the right of every child and family to appropriate material supports and the opportunity to thrive. It would also demand access to health care, including addiction and mental health services, for everyone. It would demand further that families be empowered to solve problems and seek support from the community, rather than being scapegoated and isolated.

Incremental reform efforts tend to be focused on tempering the activities of the coercive state—through greater participation by parents, additional due process protections, improvement of case practice, and so on. These are important short-term objectives, and the importance of some of them to the lives of people impacted by the system should not be underestimated. Moreover, the struggle to win reforms aimed at the coercive state can build confidence, experience, and momentum to occupy counter-hegemonic space in the elements of civil society concerned with child welfare. Real reform would connect these incremental initiatives aimed at the coercive power of the system's machinery with a broader counter-hegemonic struggle in civil society. It will also recognize that this longer-term struggle can only achieve meaningful success for those impacted by the child welfare system if it connects with counter-hegemonic struggles against racism and inequality in the war on drugs and the prison-industrial complex, housing and the control of urban space, the workplace, education, health care, and other sectors of the extended state.

A Real Paradigm Shift

One of the most overused phrases in child welfare reform—second only to "breaking the cycle"—is "paradigm shift," which is often used to describe incremental reforms. In the context of social welfare institutions, Canadian "structural social worker" Bob Mulally's analysis of paradigms is useful. Mulally defines a paradigm as consisting of an ideology, which informs an analysis of social problems, which in turn is reflected in the design of institutions, which then implement practices.[3]

The dominant neoliberal paradigm is one that attributes child neglect to personal failures, even when they are caused by poverty. There is a difference of degree, in that conservatives like William Bennett and John DiLullio say that economic poverty is caused by "moral poverty," while liberals might be inclined to acknowledge inequity and discrimination, but as contributing to the parent's failures rather than the primary problem. Both would endorse measures to regulate the poor, with the main difference being that conservatives might lean toward more straight-up punitive measures while liberals lean toward the treatment model. Both take a color-blind approach—the punitive because it purports to emphasize personal responsibility, and the treatment because it emphasizes individual pathology. Both evade the role of oppression, discrimination, and racialized poverty.

Reform efforts are typically led by professional associations, foundations, and consultants, and typically tweak or add to existing models for decision-making. Goals focus on making the system more effective at guaranteeing safety and more efficient in moving children through the pipeline, and on ensuring that services meet high standards of professional practice. At the Children's Justice Conference in 2006, the keynote address was delivered by Christine Gregoire, then governor of Washington and former child welfare worker. She stated, "Our shared goal for Washington is to improve our services by ensuring [children's] safety, promoting permanent placement for kids and supporting the well being of the entire family."[4] She went on to discuss improving educational outcomes and using data to monitor and improve services. At the 2004 National Children's Law Conference, Shay Bilchik, CEO of the Child Welfare League of America, talked about the importance of engaging communities in planning appropriately to address the needs of children in the child welfare system. She said, "We can make sure that the programs we advocate for are rooted in accurate assessment and proven practice. We can make sure that individual services are not only networked across systems, but embedded in a solid plan that has support across the community."[5] These approaches emphasize efficient service validated by research and practice, with a nod toward the confidence of the community.

The sources of private philanthropy supporting reform in child welfare suggest that conventional reform will never challenge capitalism as the cause of institutionalized childhood poverty and consequent family breakdown. The largest single funder of child welfare reform projects is the Ann E. Casey Foundation, created by the late Robert Casey, the founder of United Parcel Service (UPS). The current chair of the board of trustees is a former UPS CEO, and eight of thirteen trustees are current or former UPS corporate officers. Of the remaining trustees, one is the president of the National Board of Manufacturers, and two have backgrounds in finance. While the Casey Foundation funds high-quality research and innovative pilot activities, its perspective on the relationship of capitalism to poverty is summarized in the following introduction to an initiative to develop a "two-generation poverty-alleviation strategy": "The Casey Foundation believes that the children in greatest trouble in America today are those whose parents lack the earnings, assets, services, or social support systems required to consistently meet their families' needs. Most of these children are growing up in impoverished communities that are disconnected from the economic mainstream."[6] Thus, poverty and oppression are not essential characteristics of the capitalist system, rather "disconnection" from the "economic mainstream" is an anomaly that results in poverty and can be addressed by "fixing" families.

The language of the leading professionals and funders does not suggest any willingness to challenge the fundamental issue that relegating poor and working-class children to poverty is what makes the system in its current form necessary in the first place. It is a safety valve intended to minimize the most extreme visible harm to children of neoliberal economic policies, racism, and oppression.

A real paradigm shift would begin with the recognition that poverty is a necessary feature of capitalism, and that capitalism can't be separated from oppression based on race, class, ability, gender, and sexuality. In our analysis of child maltreatment, we would recognize that poverty causes most cases of child maltreatment, either because of lack of income and resources, or because of the stress of poverty and reduced availability of options in dealing with family issues like substance abuse, family violence, and psychiatric diagnoses. We would recognize further that the poor are at risk of state intervention because they are already subject to monitoring and intrusion by multiple systems that operate exclusively or more intensively in poor, nonwhite neighborhoods. We would recognize that bias operates at all times in how we perceive poor families, particularly those headed by single Black parents, and in how they are dealt with when they come into contact with the state.

Absent such a paradigm shift, talk of empowering the families caught up in the system and the communities in which they live will remain lip service. Thus, conferencing with community participants may become a formal prerequisite to initiating action in court, but the likelihood is that the process will be used to ratify a course of action already decided on by professionals. Real reform would change the power relationships and allow poor and working-class communities to help families solve whatever problems are threatening the welfare of their children. This needs to go beyond checking off a box labeled "community participation," and begins with supporting independent advocacy by parents who have encountered the system.

Proponents of radical change shouldn't be backed into a defensive posture, where reform is equated with a foster care agency busing a group of parents to the state capital to lobby legislators against cuts to foster care agency budgets; nor can we retreat into policy wonkdom and define change as whatever comes out of professional conferences and foundation think tanks.

Reform from Below

In New York City, the Child Welfare Organizing Project (CWOP) has a remarkable story that points out both the opportunities and challenges for real reform. CWOP began in 1994, mounting an aggressive challenge against the system, holding a candlelight vigil outside the home of Commissioner Nicholas Scoppetta on Thanksgiving in 1996 to protest newly rebranded Administration for Children's Services's reorientation toward removal. Scoppetta was the former prosecutor appointed by Mayor Giuliani, as noted in chapter 9, to fix a system plunged into crisis and scandal in large part because of Giuliani's cuts to its budget.

CWOP has had success organizing parents and training and supporting advocates, and in creating a cadre of knowledgeable, confident parent advocates who have been through CWOP's support groups and classes. It also succeeded in changing the dynamics of family conferencing in a pilot area in East Harlem. This is a small first step in the right direction.

The Fostering Positive Action (FPA) Foundation has a similar mission to organize foster parents independently of the public and private child welfare agencies to engage in self-advocacy and collective action. Importantly, FPA has a twin focus on organizing foster youth. Both CWOP and FPA show a vital recognition that change in the system will have to come from the mobilization of those living within the system rather than from the public and nonprofit bureaucracy.

CWOP and more than a dozen similar organizations nationwide have collaborated through *Rise*, a magazine published by parent activists and advocates, on a statement of rights and a plan for fundamental change in child welfare.[7] The plan consists of fifteen components, each beginning with a statement to complete the sentence, "As a parent investigated by the Child Welfare System, I have the right to . . . " (see Appendix). The first point begins with the right "not to lose my child because I'm poor," and the fifteenth with the right to "meaningful participation in developing the child welfare policies and practices that affect my family and community." Each point includes "next steps" that lay out practical demands around which parents and communities can organize. Central to the *Rise* plan is the role of parent advocates and organizers. People employed within the system should study and organize around the plan, and should demand that the professional groups and unions to which they belong do the same, because the radical change needed within the system can only come through a bottom-up approach that mobilizes parents and communities.

Global Women's Strike, which describes itself as "an international network for the recognition and payment of all caring work," has supported coordinated organizing by parents affected by foster care in two cities at opposite ends of the United States. The multiracial group DHS/DCFS Give Us Back Our Children comprises parents in Philadelphia and Los Angeles working for radical reform of their respective child welfare agencies.[8] Global Women's Strike sponsored a panel at the Left Forum in New York City in June 2014, which included representatives from these cities, as well as other parent organizers from elsewhere in the United States and in London. The panel discussed grassroots struggles in different cities, as well as commonalities and efforts to promote national and global solidarity.

ColorLines has promoted mobilizations around individual cases of undocumented parents who face deportation, with their children remaining in foster care in the United States. Just as there are important mobilizations around cases of victims of police violence and oppression, there should be further mobilizations around cases of injustice in the child welfare system. Such struggles, if they are successful, will suggest the need for further and broader struggle, and identify the economic injustice and racism that has shaped the system.

The foster care population is too small and too embattled to wage the fight alone. One encouraging note has been the participation of parents seeking radical change in the child welfare system in struggles against mass incarceration. In New York, activists who are part of an Undoing Racism in Child Welfare working group have also mobilized against stop-and-frisk and the criminalization of youth. CWOP organized a reading group for *The New Jim Crow*, in which parents explored the parallels between the criminal justice and child welfare systems.

In the current climate, conversations about changing the child welfare system can turn into radical challenges to the dominant paradigm, and perhaps the objective should be to link the struggle against child welfare as a system of social control and oppression with the struggles against mass incarceration, the war on labor, and other assaults on the working class.

What About the Social-Democratic Model?

Advocates of a greater investment in child welfare spending in the United States often draw comparisons to Scandinavia and the child welfare systems developed before the general retreat from social democratic versions of socialism as Scandinavian countries began scaling down their welfare states to make their economies more competitive in Europe. "Structural" social worker Bob Mullaly, for one, cites what he calls the "evolutionary Marxist" approach of social democracy with approval, and singles out Sweden for particular praise.[9]

In 2008, UNICEF ranked Sweden at the top of all nations surveyed in the category of child welfare. Even as neoliberalism has whittled away at the welfare state under the rule of the Christian Democrats, Sweden has not appreciably changed the child welfare system created by the Social Democrats. So is Sweden a model to be emulated?

By US standards, the array of supports provided to families is elaborate, which may reduce the demands of out-of-home care. Sweden intervenes aggressively, however, based on the relatively vague standards in its child welfare laws. There is tremendous discretion for social workers and administrators based on predictive analysis of risk factors rather than actual evidence of harm. According to Sven Hessle and Bo Vinnerljung, Swedish professors of social welfare policy, "Evidence of abuse or harm is not even a typical precondition [for removal] in practice." Instead, parental lifestyle—mainly focused on maternal alcohol or drug use—was the main factor for preschoolers placed in care in the 1980s. "Child protection legislation is diffuse and includes a high confidence in social workers' ability to make predictions of children's development."[10] Hessle and Vinnerljung cite a 1991 analysis of risk factors showing that for a child under six from a two-parent household with middle-class income whose mother had never been convicted of a crime, the risk of removal was less than one in ten thousand, while for a child in the same age range in the care of a single low-income mother without a job and a past criminal conviction the risk is one in ten. Moreover, children of immigrant backgrounds are almost twice as likely to be placed in care, a disparity mainly attributable to the overrepresentation of children of Finnish descent.[11]

Kinship placement was traditionally disfavored in Sweden because of concern among child welfare professionals about "intergenerational transmission of psychosocial problems," but a political campaign by relatives of children in care, known as the "grandma revolt," led to a change in the law in 1997.[12] Kinship placement is now supposed to be given priority.

We should also note that the Scandinavian social democratic welfare states engaged in extraordinary intervention into reproduction in developing sterilization laws and practices. In Sweden, some 35,000 eugenic sterilizations were conducted between 1934, when the Social Democratic Party passed a sterilization law, and 1975, when the policy was finally abandoned. Swedish social democratic sterilization was distinguished from Nazi eugenics in being nominally voluntary and in not being based on racial categories of hereditary unfitness, but it was still an extraordinarily expansive program, including those categorized as "feeble-minded" and those categorized as "socially unfit." In the latter category, which consisted primarily of young women of low social and economic status, were those labeled "sexually promiscuous" and "maladapted." Sterilization could be initiated by custodians of institutions, but also by community-level social workers. While the voluntary nature of eugenic sterilization was emphasized in the statutes, in practice there was coercion and deception to obtain consent. The policy was not an anomaly in the social democratic welfare state; it was seen as an important part of the bargain. Social democracy would offer an unprecedented level of material support, but would contain cost by influencing the reproduction of those deemed unfit to parent.[13]

So the top-down reformist social democratic approach offers no alternative to foster care as social control of the poor and working class. We may need to be more creative in our search for inspiration, and look to times and places where the potential for a meaningful alternative was seen, even if it was not institutionalized, and even where it was part of a class defeat.

We should look to examples like the Children's Exodus, or the brief period after the Russian Revolution when the Zhenotdel, or Women's Section, under the leadership of Alexandra Kollontai, sent a small army of organizers out to help set up childcare and communal baking and laundry arrangements in factories and villages throughout the Soviet Union.[14] The objective was engaging families and communities in identifying needs and crafting solutions. While the Zhenotdel was not uniformly successful, and operated only briefly before being overwhelmed by the devastation of the civil war and the Stalinist counterrevolution, it—like the Children's Exodus—provides a glimpse of the potential for the working class to organize to support children and families on their own terms rather than those of capital.

Cuba, even under a regime that has implemented a problematic and repressive version of socialism, has offered a model for child welfare that avoids the top-down decision-making and stigmatization of the US foster care system. Features that stand out are a separation of material needs (responsibility for which is shared with local networks) from proceedings to judge the parents' fitness to raise their children. The Minnesota State Bar Association, which is unlikely to be a nest of apologists for the Cuban Revolution, described Cuba's approach to child welfare:

> Cuban child welfare law seems to make it very hard to be a bad parent; community-based child welfare nets, including schools and neighborhoods, are active in child-rearing. Removal of a child from biological parents is rare and typically occurs only where the parent has committed a crime against the child or has behavioral problems. In such situations, grandparents can obtain custody of the child. The Cuban child welfare system also provides protection for orphans and abandoned children, although the latter are quite uncommon.[15]

There will continue to be a need for intervention to protect children whose safety or health is jeopardized, even when the root causes of the threats relate to poverty and the forms of oppression are inseparable from capitalism. For the foreseeable future, it will be necessary to work to minimize the extent that poverty is equated with bad parenting, promote reform that strengthens the role of families and communities when intervention must occur, confront bias and institutionalized racism within the child welfare system, and support organizing and activism among parents, foster parents, foster youth, and front-line workers. In the latter endeavor, we should look for opportunities to build linkages between all the families, individuals, and communities affected by the system.

Child Welfare Under Socialism?

Even a complete restructuring of social and economic relationships under socialism would not eliminate the need for intervention, including out-of-home care. Such change would, however, make it possible to address exploitation and chronic unemployment, lack of adequate housing, shortages of health care and childcare, and the problems associated with mass incarceration.

Because impoverishment of a substantial portion of the population would no longer be a necessary feature of the economic order, the stresses and insecurity that manifest in family breakdown would also begin to abate. Fewer and fewer children would be living in circumstances that would make intervention likely. Such change, moreover, would eliminate capital's need for "soft police" (less coercive agents of the state from social service professions) to monitor and control poor and working-class families of color, just as it would eliminate the need for "hard police" (explicitly coercive agents of the state to enforce the laws) to maintain the economic elite.

Just as communities would be able to separate collective efforts to maintain public order and safety from class control and racial oppression, they would also separate child safety and well-being from these state roles. Addressing the ravages of capitalism on children, especially children of color, would change the scale and nature of the child welfare system.

As Engels argued, the state is needed as "an organization of the . . . exploiting class, for the maintenance of its external conditions of production, and, therefore, especially, for the purpose of forcibly keeping the exploited classes in the condition of oppression corresponding with the given mode of production."[16] When the state ceases to function in that role, it ceases to exist in its current form, and is no longer the state as we recognize it based on our experience.

New possibilities will open up for organizing to meet social needs. In the realm of child welfare, it will be possible to envision completely different ways of solving the problems of families, without the need for large public and nongovernmental bureaucracies to administer out-of-home care, and courts to maintain a layer of due process. Instead, a much smaller, less punitive system will develop through the efforts of neighbors, extended family, and providers of health care, mental health services, parenting support, and child-care to identify and address cases of child maltreatment that might still occur.

TEN

Child Welfare and Social Reproduction

Why Is Social Reproduction Relevant to Child Welfare?

Several times in the earlier chapters, we have encountered the Marxist concept of social reproduction, which deals with the important service families perform for capitalism in raising new workers. I maintain that social reproduction is vital in understanding a system that makes it its business to regulate poor and working-class families. To make that point, it's necessary to delve into the fundamentals of Marxist economics generally and social reproduction specifically, and then link these concepts to the operation of the child welfare system as I've described it.

Social reproduction links the production of goods and services with the reproduction of human workers. Social reproduction provides a crucial basis for the regulation of poor and working-class family life. This regulation is accomplished in many ways, including through policies affecting public education, the tax code, and other areas of public policy. The child welfare system is one of a number of mechanisms with some similarity of purpose in providing for youth (schools, health care, and so on), but it is the one in which the power of the state and civil society is exercised most unambiguously.

The Nuts and Bolts of Social Reproduction

To understand social reproduction, it is necessary to begin with the model of wage labor under capitalism, to show how the bringing up of a new generation of workers is a basic need of capitalism. This is the case even when parents are disconnected to one degree or another from wage labor. For our purposes, we can summarize the model in its simplest terms.

Under capitalism, the wage of workers has the effect of commodifying labor. Like any commodity, labor has both "use value" (the benefit realized by the employer who consumes it in production) and "exchange value" (measured by the exchange of wages). Labor is distinguished from everything else that takes commodity form in that the use value ordinarily exceeds the exchange value, creating the surplus value, which allows for profit and the creation of more capital to invest in production. Obviously, capitalists have an incentive to ensure that the value of labor is as low as possible to retain a larger use value, with the difference being the "surplus value."

Labor is an input in the production process, and, like machinery, must be replaced when it is no longer fit for the purpose. Replacement can occur through immigration, movement of enterprises to new labor markets, or expansion of the labor market to include groups previously excluded. Invariably, however, it includes children of workers or potential workers growing up and entering the workforce. To ensure this process, the wage paid to workers must not only be sufficient to keep the workers alive and strong enough to produce but to sustain the children of the workers who will eventually replace them in the workforce. Value should not, therefore, be lower than is necessary to sustain the worker to produce the next generation of workers destined to replace their parents in the workforce.[1]

Capitalists and workers have very different ideas about what constitutes the necessary wage to meet the basic needs of the worker and the children of the worker. Complex variables affect the willingness of workers to insist on higher wages, and their ability to prevail, and the necessary level of subsistence varies widely according to time and place. As Lise Vogel explains: "When business is good, needs and consumption—the worker's 'share of civilization'—expand. In the long run, capital's drive for accumulation has the tendency to permit the worker to augment and replace 'natural' needs with 'historically created' ones."[2]

Thus, the consensus about what constitutes a "living wage" is variable, depending on time and place. The expected standard of living tends to incorporate the cost of supporting children, because of the expectation that workers are solely responsible for their children. So while capitalism relies on workers to create and nurture their replacements, support for that endeavor is provided primarily through the wage negotiated for the provision of labor.

Marx and Engels recognized that the social relationships of family had evolved over time in response to changes in the dominant mode of production. Marx describes the manner in which "labor-power" is sold as a commodity for a sum representing not just subsistence, but replacement:

> The owner of labour-power is mortal. If then his appearance in the market is to be continuous, and the continuous conversion of money into capital assumes this, the seller of labour-power must perpetuate himself, "in the way that every living individual perpetuates himself, by procreation." The labour-power withdrawn from the market by wear and tear and death, must be continually replaced by, at the very least, an equal amount of fresh labour-power. Hence the sum of the means of subsistence necessary for the production of labour-power must include the means necessary for the labourer's substitutes, i.e., his children, in order that this race of peculiar commodity-owners may perpetuate its appearance in the market.[3]

Part of the function of workers under capitalism, therefore, is to provide for the replacement of their labor-power through procreation and child-rearing.

Engels examined family through pre-history and history, and the relationship of changes in structure and gender roles to changes in property rights and production:

> With the patriarchal family, and still more with the single monogamous family, a change came. Household management lost its public character. It no longer concerned society. It became a private service; the wife became the head servant, excluded from all participation in social production. Not until the coming of modern large-scale industry was the road to social production

opened to her again—and then only to the proletarian wife. But it was opened in such a manner that, if she carries out her duties in the private service of her family, she remains excluded from public production and unable to earn; and if she wants to take part in public production and earn independently, she cannot carry out family duties. And the wife's position in the factory is the position of women in all branches of business, right up to medicine and the law. The modern individual family is founded on the open or concealed domestic slavery of the wife, and modern society is a mass composed of these individual families as its molecules.[4]

Under precapitalist systems, production centered around the home and the family, and gender roles and family structure were idealized to reflect those needs. As production moved away from the home, the division of labor and idealized structure of the family evolved around the nuclear family's role as furnishing wage labor outside the home and raising the next generation of workers. Sharon Smith encapsulates the idea very concisely:

> The nuclear family remains a system for privatized reproduction. . . . [R]uling class families produce the next ruling class, and working families produce the next generation of workers. . . . [T]oday's capitalists take precious little responsibility for the legion of workers whose labor produces their profits. . . . The working-class family is extremely valuable to the capitalist system as a cheap means of reproducing labor power. The large-scale entry of working-class women into the workforce hasn't changed that fact. Working-class women are expected to do both.[5]

There are features of capitalism that help to maintain downward pressure of wages, and none is more crucial than the "reserve army of labor." Capitalism depends on expansion of the laboring population for two reasons. One is because the use value of labor creates surplus value, and thus is essential for the growth of capital. The other is that is necessary to maintain a workforce that contains workers whose labor is not actually needed at the moment. These "superfluous" workers can be brought into the active workforce when needed, and can also be used to hold down wages.[6]

The concept of a reserve army suggests a homogenous group of potential laborers waiting for the call, but there is actually rigid stratification. As Vogel wrote:

> At all times . . . relative surplus population takes several distinct forms. The floating reserve is made up of workers who move in and out of employment according to the needs of the constantly changing capitalist labour process. The latent reserve consists of those thrust out of work by the extension of capitalism into non-capitalist sectors. The stagnant reserve is formed by chronically under-employed workers, who are condemned to terrible poverty and always willing to work for the lowest wages in the worst conditions. Below these three categories of reserves, paupers make up the bottom layer of the surplus-population. "Pauperism," Marx observes, "is the hospital of the active labor army and the dead weight of the industrial reserve army."[7]

Poverty therefore, is neither a failure of capitalism nor an incidental side effect; it is necessary for capitalism to thrive. Equally important, segments of the population are kept permanently unemployed or underemployed, and are unlikely to benefit during periods of expansion of the active workforce. In the United States, Blacks are disproportionately represented among those with the least stable connections to employment. Since the Bureau of Labor Statistics began disaggregating employment data by race in 1954, Black unemployment has been on average more than twice that of whites. When unemployment has been falling, moreover, Blacks who were previously considered "non-participants" in the workforce have been the very last to be hired, generally joining the boom only shortly before a downturn in the business cycle. When the downturn occurs, Blacks are the first to absorb job losses.[8] Indigenous people in the United States have the lowest rate of labor force participation and an unemployment rate about double the national average.[9] Latinos have rates of unemployment lower than those for Blacks and indigenous people, but higher than for whites and Asians, and a high rate of poverty concentrated among the youngest and oldest Latinos.[10]

While gradations of poverty are essential to capitalism, including capitalism under a representative democracy, systemic racialized poverty also creates challenges to capitalism. One is the implicit threat that those marginalized and impoverished will disrupt society through violence or resistance. A variety of mechanisms have to be constructed to regulate and control the poor, from aggressive, increasingly militarized policing to mass incarceration and carefully controlled schools that look different than the schools attended by students from affluent families to intervention into family life. Another challenge is the threat to legitimacy if the relationship of poverty to capitalism is recognized for what it is. It is necessary to create and maintain an ideology that blames the poor for their condition. This is especially the case when the issue at hand is the conditions under which poor children are growing up.

So as we have seen, capitalism requires that workers be replaced by a new generation, but also requires that some workers are relegated to the reserve army of labor and an impoverished existence that makes it extraordinarily difficult to provide for the material needs of children. The tension between these two requirements of capitalism means that capitalism both imposes poverty and polices the poor. Most immediately, it is necessary to be seen to be protecting children from the most extreme effects of poverty and to situate blame with parents when children are actually harmed or placed at risk of harm. A longer-term objective is to ensure that the children of the poor remain of potential use in the labor market.

The idealization of the nuclear family is very much in the interest of capitalism, as is the expectation that working-class families will be able to simultaneously provide labor under exploitive conditions while reproducing their labor power in the form of children. So as a general proposition, state intervention to regulate working-class families is justified to enforce those expectations.

The disparate treatment of poor families subject to state surveillance and control and middle- and upper-class families left to their own devises is enshrined in law. In the Clinton-era Adoption and Safe Families Act (ASFA), for example, if a child has remained in foster care for fifteen out of twenty-two months and the agency can show it has made diligent efforts to reunite the family, the system is supposed to move toward terminating parental rights in order to "free" the child for adoption. This is because ASFA's prioritization of "permanency" outweighs any residual attachment the child may have to the parent from whom she is separated. In the case of divorce law, there is no similar devaluing of a child's relationship to a noncustodial parent. Thus, a noncustodial parent who visits a child once a week for years on end pursuant to a custody agreement has rights that will be respected and enforced under the law, while a parent who visits a child at a foster care agency once a week will be said to have a relationship too tenuous to be protected once fifteen months have elapsed. This is because laws written specifically to regulate poor families are far less deferential to family ties.

Americans are unwilling to admit that as a nation, the United States is strikingly indifferent to the welfare of children, as evidenced by the 2013 UNICEF report ranking the United States thirty-fourth of thirty-five nations (edged out of last place by Romania) in childhood poverty. The belief in the superiority of US society—enshrined in the doctrine of "American exceptionalism"—complicates the way childhood poverty is discussed.

One factor is that the United States is by far the most religious among wealthy nations. Nearly 60 percent of Americans polled say that religion—overwhelmingly Christianity—is "very important" in their lives.[11] By contrast, in Finland, which had the lowest level of childhood poverty in the UNICEF study, only about 2 percent of church members attend services regularly, and only third of Finns report a belief in God.[12] Americans, therefore, nominally pledge adherence to the notion in the gospels that they should be judged by their treatment of the "least among us," while simultaneously tolerating rates of childhood poverty unknown in other countries with the resources to do something about it.

The United States is not alone in seeking to place blame on parents for the consequences of childhood poverty, but the combination of religiosity and hegemonic belief in the moral superiority of "American values" makes it especially important ideologically. Deflection of blame to parents may take the form of moralism, as when comedian Bill Cosby said in 2004, "The lower economic people are not holding up their end in this deal. These people are not parenting."[13] Alternatively, it may be cast in terms of "treatment" offered to pathological families. Often, moral and clinical explanations are intertwined, and both invoke personal responsibility and growth as a solution to the problems of childhood poverty.

The ideological narratives extend well beyond the child welfare system, as exemplified by the Bill Cosby example, but the child welfare system is where these narratives are put into practice most aggressively. It follows that one way in which the system meets the needs of capitalism is by deflecting the threat to legitimacy posed by racialized child poverty.

As a concept of Marxist political economy, social reproduction is extremely useful in explaining the motivation for intervention into poor and working-class families in the child welfare system and in other areas in which coercive or ideological power is wielded by the state and by nongovernmental organizations and private business interests. Historically, social reproduction can add to our understanding of a number of attacks leveled against poor and working-class people as parents or potential parents. Judgments about fitness to parent are of concern to the class controlling capital first and foremost because of capital's interest in the output of social reproduction.

The most extreme—in fact, genocidal—attack was the eugenics movement that began in the late nineteenth century and continued openly until World War II and much more circumspectly thereafter. A network of researchers and generators of policy, financed by the largesse of wealthy donors, constructed a pseudoscientific theory of genetically transmitted "pauperism" and "feeble-mindedness" backed by fraudulent data constructed to validate the theory. Eugenics, especially in the United States, was inextricably linked to racism and xenophobia, but poor native-born whites were also targeted, so the class hatred was not strictly limited by racism or hostility toward immigrants. The network also cultivated fear of an accelerating, existential threat to the "superior racial stock" of white Americans. With eugenics, the interference with family life took the extreme form of forced sterilization and anti-miscegenation laws that denied or regulated the opportunity many poor Americans had to parent.[14]

Looked at in terms of the social reproduction function of child-rearing, eugenics seems less like a historical anomaly borne of bad ideas (racism, xenophobia, disability oppression) meeting mad scientists and more like an attempt by industrial capitalism to rationalize and regulate human reproduction in its own interest. The child welfare system in its formative years was neither as extreme nor as ambitious as the eugenics movement, but the parallels are important. Wealthy donors and middle-class operatives, motivated by a mixture of class fear and sense of noblesse oblige, adopted the mission of intervening in the reproductive and family lives of poor and working-class people, ostensibly for the greater good. In both cases, they molded laws and policies and ultimately shaped how and against whom the coercive power of the state would be used.

ELEVEN

Socialism and the Parent-Child Relationship

A Challenge for Marxists

While the theory of social reproduction can add to our understanding of why the child welfare system exists in its current form, which is crucial to identifying goals for reform and transformation, there is a challenge in introducing Marxist concepts into a conversation about child welfare. Struggles within the child welfare system involve efforts by those subject to its control to protect and preserve their relationships to their children. At times, Marxists have expressed thoughts about the role of the family under capitalism in language that suggests Marxists look forward to a future when families are essentially collectivized. One reason is the often heavy-handed and confusing language used in some very important writing by Marxist theorists, beginning with Marx and Engels themselves. Another is the fact that, while considerable effort has gone into properly explaining and contextualizing the writings of Marx, Engels, and others relative to the oppression of women within the family, much less has been written about the parent-child relationship. Finally, there is the selective quotation and willful distortion by many on the right, who have been leveling inflammatory charges against Marxism as hostile to family and religion for more than a century.

From the early writings of Marx and Engels, there are passages that helped to develop an understanding of the family and its relationship to production, its transformation under capitalism, and its role in the oppression of women. In *Theses on Feuerbach*, written in 1845, Marx and Engels wrote, "[O]nce the earthly family is discovered to be the secret of the holy family, the former must then itself be destroyed in theory and in practice."[1] In *The German Ideology*, they note that "the supersession of individual economy is inseparable from the supersession of the family."[2] In *The Principles of Communism* in 1847, Engels includes the following catechism:

> Question 21: What influence will the communist order of society have upon the family?
>
> Answer: It will make the relation between the sexes a purely private relation which concerns only the person involved, and in which society has no call to interfere. It is able to do this because it abolishes private property and educates children communally, thus destroying the twin foundations of hitherto existing marriage—the dependence through private property of the wife upon the husband and of the children upon the parents.[3]

On first reading, these and other quotes suggest that the tenets of Marxism include a normative judgment rejecting family relations. A few things need to be kept in mind, however. The criticism of Marxism as antifamily fails to note that a consensus eventually developed among liberals that a transformation of family was necessary to begin to address the oppression of women. Thus, few people attacking the early calls for transformation in the Marxist tradition would in fact defend the family as it existed in the time of Marx and Engels. Few would defend the idea that a husband is legally the owner of his wife's labor and the labor of minor children, and therefore able to make decisions about whether and where they work and how their income is used. So the family relationships Marx and Engels criticized no longer exist as a matter of law in the countries with which they were familiar.

In addition, Marx and Engels were convinced that proletarian families would be unable to survive the conditions of industrial capitalism, specifically the tendency to draw women and children into wage labor. They believed, therefore, that the relationships within the working-class family were in the process of being destroyed, so talking about its transformation was not a rejection of family relationships as such, but a recognition that change was inevitable, and that socialism would feature very different relationships. In *The Communist Manifesto* in 1848, Marx and Engels write:

> Abolition of the family! Even the most radical flare up at this infamous proposal of the communists.
>
> On what foundation is the present family, the bourgeois family, based? On capital, on private gain. In its completely developed form, this family exists only among the bourgeoisie. But this state of things finds its complement in the practical absence of the family among the proletarians, and in public prostitution.
>
> The bourgeois family will vanish as a matter of course when its complement vanishes, and both will vanish with the vanishing of capitalism. . . .
>
> The bourgeois clap-trap about the family and education, about the hallowed co-relation of parent and child, become all the more disgusting when all the proletarian family ties are severed by the action of modern industry, and their children are transformed into simple articles of commerce and instruments of labor.[4]

A Higher Form of Family

Marx and Engels underestimated the resiliency of family ties, or perhaps the extent to which the resistance to child labor in industry would be successful at preventing the destruction of the family. In addition, while they didn't expand on their meaning, there is some difficulty interpreting their description of the destruction of family. As Heather Brown points out, the German word that has been translated in different works as "abolition," "transformation," and "destruction," is *"aufhebung,"* which doesn't have a simple literal translation into English. It suggests something other than simple destruction and replacement in a linear sense. What Marx and Engels seem to have been thinking of is a dialectical process whereby "the oppressive aspects of the family are dissolved but the positive elements are incorporated into a new type of family structure."[5] Thus, used in the sense of "transformation," or "positive supersession," the concept suggests a new existence for family relationships freed of the oppression of women and the dictates of capitalist production.

Indeed, in *Capital*, Marx refers to a "higher form of family" that would survive the subordination of women.[6] Earlier, in the *1844 Philosophical and Economic Manuscripts*, first published more than four decades after his death, Marx describes the need for the transformation not only of family but of all social institutions following the abolition of private property. The relationships of capitalism lead to alienation of the worker from the product of labor because once the product takes the form of commodity with exchange value belonging to the employer, labor loses its quality for the workers of expressing human purpose and creativity: "Work is *external* to the worker, that it is not part of his nature; and that, consequently, he does not fulfill himself in his work but denies himself, has a feeling of misery rather than well being, does not develop freely his mental and physical energies, but is physically exhausted and mentally debased. The worker therefore feels himself at home only during his leisure time, whereas at work he feels himself homeless."[7]

Marx believed however, that even in leisure time, workers could not find full expression of their humanity. The worker, he writes, "feels himself to be freely active only in his animal functions—eating, drinking and procreating, or at most also in his dwelling and in personal adornment—while in his human functions he is reduced to an animal. . . . Eating, drinking and procreating are of course also genuine human functions. But abstractly considered, apart from the environment of other human activities, and turned into final and sole ends, they are animal functions."[8]

Thus, while alienation begins with the labor process, it does not follow that simply abolishing the property relationships of capitalism would change all other social relationships. It would, however, open the door to the transformation of those relationships. As Marx wrote, "Religion, the family, the state, law, morality, science, art, and so on, are only *particular* forms of production and come under its general law. The positive transcendence of *private property* as the appropriation of *human* life, is therefore the positive transcendence of all estrangement—that is to say, the return of man from religion, family, state, etc., to his *human*, i.e. *social*, existence."[9]

For Engels, who focused much more narrowly on the function of family in guaranteeing succession of property rights, which is largely irrelevant for wage laborers possessing no property, the discussion of transformation seems more simplistic and mechanical. In *The Origin of the Family, Private Property and the State*, published in 1884, Engels states that once family is no longer fulfilling an economic function, "private housekeeping is transformed into a social industry . . . and the care and education of the children becomes a public affair."[10] As noted, Engels had earlier declared that under the "communistic order" the relations between men and women would become "a purely private relation which concerns only the persons involved." While he recognizes that relationships between adult family members would be transformed in a positive way, he gives little indication what he thinks a continuing parent-child relationship would be like.

It is appropriate that neither Marx nor Engels attempted to prescribe the nature of family under socialism. Each seemed to believe that there was some "natural" division of labor by gender in the household, but they recognized that social relationships would reflect the needs of the participants freed from the limits of the capitalist system of production. While they apparently could not envision what families would look like when liberated from gender oppression and the material burden of creating the next generation of workers, they nevertheless recognized that families would exist in forms of their own choosing.

Kollontai, Communism, and the Family

Marxist theory advanced to a more concrete consideration of the transformation of the family with the Russian Revolution and the coming to power of the Bolsheviks. The Bolsheviks sought to liberate women from the legal constraints and state of domestic servitude that had been their lot under the tsar. The work of Alexandra Kollontai, first as commissar of social welfare and later as a deputy director and then director of the Zhenotdel, the women's department of the Communist Party, provides the best account of how these issues played out under the extraordinarily difficult circumstances of the revolution and civil war. Kollontai was also witness to the abandonment of efforts to eliminate the oppression of women in the home under the Stalinist counterrevolution.

Kollontai and other Bolsheviks encountered resistance from working-class women, both from the massive peasant class and the much smaller proletariat. Despite the crushing burden of work outside and inside the home, and the desperate need for material support for mothers, the women were wary of talk of communal kitchens, childcare, and so on. At a congress in Moscow in November 1918, more than a thousand delegates gathered for the First All Russian Congress of Working and Peasant Women. They were supporters of the revolution and committed to improving the political and material condition of women, but their initial response to a proposal for community childcare was to shout down the speaker with cries of, "We won't give up our children!"[11] Kollontai spoke next, and a revised version of her speech was later published as *Communism and the Family*. She began by posing the questions, "Will the family continue to exist under communism? Will the family remain in the same form? These questions are troubling many women of the working class and troubling their menfolk as well."[12] She noted the weakening of families under capitalism, and that working-class parents had little time to spend with their children because of the need to work as many hours as possible to provide for their material needs. She talked about the need for the new society to provide for the material needs of children, and the benefits of freely available childcare, family meals, community laundries, and other supports. But she offered reassurance to the "worker-mothers" that their children were not to be taken away to be raised by the state:

> Working mothers have no need to be alarmed; communists are not intending to take children away from their parents or to tear the baby from the breast of its mother, and neither is it planning to take violent measures to destroy the family. No such thing! The aims of communist society are quite different. Communist

society sees that the old type of family is breaking up, and that all the old pillars which supported the family as a social unit are being removed: the domestic economy is dying, and working-class parents are unable to take care of their children or provide them with sustenance and education. Parents and children suffer equally from this situation. Communist society has this to say to the working woman and working man: "You are young, you love each other. Everyone has the right to happiness. Therefore live your life. Do not flee happiness. Do not fear marriage, even though under capitalism marriage was truly a chain of sorrow. Do not be afraid of having children. Society needs more workers and rejoices at the birth of every child. You do not have to worry about the future of your child; your child will know neither hunger nor cold." Communist society takes care of every child and guarantees both him and his mother material and moral support. Society will feed, bring up and educate the child. At the same time, those parents who desire to participate in the education of their children will by no means be prevented from doing so. Communist society will take upon itself all the duties involved in the education of the child, but the joys of parenthood will not be taken away from those who are capable of appreciating them. Such are the plans of communist society and they can hardly be interpreted as the forcible destruction of the family and the forcible separation of child from mother.[13]

What Kollontai is suggesting is a richer family life. Previously, parents carried the often unsupportable burden of responsibility for all of their children's material needs, even though the primary beneficiary is the capitalist class that owns the means of production. When society both owns the means of production and provides for the material support of the next generation, parents are free to enjoy the human—rather than economic—parent-child relationship. In addition, Kollontai maintains that in such a society, the larger community would be engaged in the raising of children:

> The woman who takes up the struggle for the liberation of the working class must learn to understand that there is no more room for the old proprietary attitude that says: "These are my children, I owe them all my maternal solicitude and affection;

those are your children, they are no concern of mine and I don't care if they go hungry and cold—I have no time for other children." The worker-mother must learn not to differentiate between yours and mine; she must remember that there are only our children, the children of Russia's communist workers.[14]

The suspicion that socialists aim toward the destruction of families has been persistent. Kollontai faced that accusation before and during the revolution and civil war, and the right has tried to perpetuate the myth, even trying to blame the social breakdown in present-day neoliberal Russia on the Bolsheviks' alleged attacks on traditional families.[15] In 1922, a federal bill aimed at reducing infant mortality by funding maternal and child health centers was opposed by a right-wing group called the Woman Patriots as a plot to "Bolshevize" America by destroying the family.[16] In 1963, a Florida congressman read into the Congressional Record an excerpt of a book called *The Naked Communist* by Cleon Skousen, which included Skousen's formulation of the forty-five goals of communism. Among them were:

40. Discredit the family as an institution. Encourage promiscuity and easy divorce.

41. Emphasize the need to raise children away from the negative influence of parents. Attribute prejudices, mental blocks and retarding of children to suppressive influence of parents.[17]

Interestingly, the attack from anticommunists more or less echoes criticism Kollontai encountered once the Stalinist counterrevolution had begun to roll back the early Bolshevik reforms. In 1936, as the regime recriminalized homosexuality, tightened divorce laws, and restricted the right to abortion, Kollontai was attacked as promoting the abolition of families in favor of promiscuity for adults and state care for children.[18]

In the short term, of course, most of our conversation will be about reforms—reducing the intrusiveness, disempowerment, and discriminatory impact of state intervention, and providing material supports from the state to families in a non-punitive, non-infantilizing manner. Nevertheless, socialists need to learn to discuss the possibility of family life under socialism in positive terms. Often, the discussion is incomplete, in focusing on the responsibilities of which families would be relieved. Poor and working-class families, however, are used to fighting constant battles to protect and preserve their families against the assaults of the capitalist state and economy. The assaults on Black families have been particularly vicious. Struggles in child welfare are perhaps the most dramatic example, but virtually all workers struggle to find more time for their family life. Thus simply talking about socialized childcare as relieving families of their role in social reproduction will be threatening to people who are still fighting for and on behalf of their children.

A narrative that points toward the possibility of richer family life based on the wishes of family members rather than economic obligation needs to be developed. The separation of material needs from family relationships should be liberating for families, and the parent-child relationship should thrive. In addition, a more expansive community participation in child-rearing should open up possibilities for greater support for children and parents and an extension of family life beyond the nuclear family as an economic unit. The point is not to be prescriptive, but to emphasize that greater freedom and possibility is possible when families are not governed by capitalism. Kollontai made such arguments—albeit in dated language—and her writings and work should be studied to help develop responses appropriate to the current context to the questions that arise concerning what Marxism really has to say about families and children.

Acknowledgments

Many people contributed to this book long before I ever had an inkling that there would *be* a book, beginning with many workers and advocates in the child welfare system who helped me get my bearings when I arrived for a one-year sojourn that turned into one more than a decade and counting. I must thank many individuals who helped me when I began to explore connections between capitalism and the system I found myself a part of, but I can only begin to identify them by name. Friends and colleagues encouraged me to write on the topic, including Nordia Nelson Shackleford and Regina Schaeffer, who read and commented on an early draft of the article that was the genesis of this book. As I began to develop the arguments that now form the book, my colleagues in the Education Unit at ACS (now grandiloquently rechristened the Office of Education Support and Policy Planning): Roberto Romero, Nancy Santiago, Melissa Cueto, Chris Tan, and Kathleen Hoskins were willing to engage in discussions that refined and sharpened my analysis.

Folks at the Child Welfare Organizing Project agreed to help me develop the first of three panels on child welfare at the Left Forum, and I learned a great deal from our discussions, so I'd like to thank Allison Brown, Sandra Killett, Mike Arsham, and Jovonna Freison. Jovonna has been an inspirational and humbling presence each time I've appeared publicly with her. Seth Wessler of *ColorLines* also appeared on that first panel, and Doreen Matthews of Fostering Positive Action, Rolando Bini of Parents in Action, and Dave Bliven (a lawyer representing parents), appeared on subsequent panels. I learned something from each of them.

An embryonic version of this book appeared in an article in the *International Socialist Review*, and various people at the *ISR* and its periphery read and edited drafts, or otherwise helped to push it forward for publication, including, in egalitarian alphabetical order, Paul D'Amato, Jason Farbman, Brian Jones, Danny Katch, John McDonald, Jen Roesch, Keith Rosenthal, Lance Selfa, Ahmed Shawki, Ashley Smith, and Sherry Wolf.

At Haymarket Books, I would like to thank Anthony Arnove, Nisha Bolsey, Julie Fain, and, of course, the editors who worked on the manuscript. Alison McKenna identified a propensity on my part to overstate my criticism of professionals in the system, and her informed critique resulted in many important modifications, even if they didn't fully resolve every difference over a subject about which we both hold strong opinions. I appreciate her contribution. Annie Zirin made incredibly useful suggestions for clarification and greater accessibility, and I greatly appreciate her contributions and enthusiasm for the book. And Dao X. Tran has been a great friend, advocate, and editor from the first, which is why she has earned, in addition to my lasting gratitude, a long-promised key lime pie.

My coworkers at Sinergia were extremely supportive when I needed to take scattered vacation days to work on the book. Any Nuñez, Lore Barcelona, Rebecca Maitin, and Yesenia Estrella, in particular, helped to ensure that my absences were disconcertingly inconsequential. Yesenia was also a focus group of one when I had to quickly come up with a new title, and gently pooh-poohed a number of truly bad ideas before I adapted the quote from Malcolm X for the present title.

I would also like to thank my wife, Monica Johnson, LMSW, who has been waiting for the book to go to press so she can find out if I really savaged her profession as much as I kept telling her I did. (I didn't.) She also barely mentioned my leaving the living room half-painted for months while I worked on the manuscript, which was a great help. Kristian and Katelyn, who will replace us both in the workforce when we are worn out, were also very understanding about late nights and weekends spent working on the book. I owe them a trip to Disney World, although that may hasten the previously mentioned wearing-out process.

Finally, I would like to dedicate this book to the memory of my brother Rich, of Local 333 of the United Marine Division of the International Organization of Masters, Mates & Pilots and the International Longshoremen's Association, who died while I was finishing the book. We miss him.

From Rights to Reality*

A Plan for Parent Advocacy and Family-Centered Child Welfare Reform

From Rights to Reality is designed to unite parents and parent advocacy around a common set of goals. It identifies fifteen rights for parents affected by the child welfare system. Most parents do not yet have these rights in child welfare proceedings. From Rights to Reality represents a commitment to working in our communities and nationwide to make these rights a reality.

As a parent investigated by the child welfare system:

1. I HAVE THE RIGHT TO not lose my child because I'm poor.

2. I HAVE THE RIGHT TO services that will support me in raising my child at home.

3. I HAVE THE RIGHT TO speak for myself and be heard at every step of the child protective service process.

4. I HAVE THE RIGHT TO be informed of my rights.

5. I HAVE THE RIGHT TO a meaningful and fair hearing before my parental rights are limited in any way.

6. I HAVE THE RIGHT TO quality legal representation.

---

* Originally published in *Rise: Stories by and for Parents Affected by the Child Welfare System*; see www.risemagazine.org/PDF/From_Rights_to_Reality.pdf.

7. I HAVE THE RIGHT TO support from someone who has been in my shoes.

8. I HAVE THE RIGHT TO have my child quickly placed with someone I trust.

9. I HAVE THE RIGHT TO frequent, meaningful contact with my child.

10. I HAVE THE RIGHT TO make decisions about my child's life in care.

11. I HAVE THE RIGHT TO privacy.

12. I HAVE THE RIGHT TO fair treatment regardless of my race, culture, gender, or religion.

13. I HAVE THE RIGHT TO services that will support me in reunifying with my child.

14. I HAVE THE RIGHT TO offer my child a lifelong relationship.

15. I HAVE THE RIGHT TO meaningful participation in developing the child welfare policies and practices that affect my family and community.

Notes

Introduction

1. Reliable data is not available to quantify the extent to which the primary functions of the child welfare system have been assumed by for-profit entities, although chapter 8 will detail state-specific privatization initiatives assigning these core functions (investigation and child protection, foster care administration) to for-profits. It is a trend that has considerable ideological pull for many elected officials, and therefore bears careful scrutiny and caution, just as charter schools had an ideological and portentous importance even when very small numbers of students in widely dispersed jurisdictions were attending them. Beyond wholesale assumption of hitherto public core functions, for-profits have emerged as an outgrowth of the growing prominence of "evidence-based models" in the treatment of families, children, and youth. While evidence-based practice has undeniable positive aspects for the system and for families, it has also created the opportunity for model developers, often associated with universities, to create for-profit subsidiaries to sell training and consultation services to public and not-for-profit entities across the country, often shifting control from the local level to far-flung consultants monitoring services for "fidelity to the model."

2. Child Trends Data Bank, "Foster Care: Indicators on Children and Youth," December 2014, 3, www.childtrends.org/wp-content/uploads/2014/07/12_Foster_Care.pdf.

3. New York City Administration for Children's Services, "Update Five-Year Trend FY 2005–FY 2009," www.nyc.gov/html/acs/downloads/pdf/stats_5_year_2009.pdf.

4. "How Race, Poverty and Foster Care Are Connected," *Milwaukee Journal-Sentinel*, December 25, 2008, www.jsonline.com/news/opinion/36703034.html.

5. Andrea Sedlak, et al., "Fourth National Incidence Report on Child Abuse and Neglect [NIS-4]: Report to Congress," U.S. Department of Health and Human Services, 2006, http://www.acf.hhs.gov/sites/default/files/opre/nis4_report_congress_full_pdf_jan2010.pdf; and Andrea J. Sedlak, Karla McPherson, and Barnali Das, "Supplementary Analyses

of Race Differences in Child Maltreatment Rates in the [NIS-4]," U.S. Department of Health and Human Services, 2010, 1.

6. Tina Lee, *Catching a Case: Inequality and Fear in New York City's Child Welfare System* (New Brunswick, NJ: Rutgers University Press, 2016), 130.

7. Brookings Institute, "Adoption from Foster Care: Aiding Children While Saving Public Money," 2011, www.brookings.edu/research/reports/2011/05/adoption-foster-care-zill.

8. Lee, *Catching a Case*, 4.

9. Max Fisher, "Map: How 35 Countries Compare on Child Poverty (the U.S. Is Ranked 34th)," *WorldView, Washington Post*, April 15, 2013, www.washingtonpost.com/blogs/worldviews/wp/2013/04/15/map-how-35-countries-compare-on-child-poverty-the-u-s-is-ranked-34th/.

Chapter One: The "Orphan Trains"—Then and Now

1. Quoted in Steven O'Connor, *Orphan Trains: The Story of Charles Loring Brace and the Children He Saved and Failed* (New York: Houghton Mifflin, 2001), 84.

2. The account of the Children's Exodus is based generally on Bruce Watson, *Bread and Roses: Migrants and the Struggle for the American Dream* (New York: Viking, 2005), 141–79.

3. Seth Freed Wessler, "Shattered Families: The Perilous Intersection of Immigration Enforcement and the Child Welfare System," Applied Research Center, November 2011, http://act.colorlines.com/acton/attachment/1069/f-007a/0/-/-/-/-/file.pdf; Seth Freed Wessler, "Thousands of Kids Lost from Parents in U.S. Deportation System," November 2, 2011, http://colorlines.com/archives/2011/11/thousands_of_kids_lost_in_foster_homes_after_parents_deportation.html.

4. Laura Sullivan, "Incentives and Cultural Bias Fuel Foster System," National Public Radio, October 25, 2011, www.npr.org/2011/10/25/141662357/incentives-and-cultural-bias-fuel-foster-system.

5. Carrie Rickey, "Gingrich's 'Boys Town' Solution: Social Policy Meets Movie Nostalgia. The Film Was Made in 1938. Things Aren't That Simple Today, Professionals Say," *Philly.com*, December 6, 1994, http://articles.philly.com/1994-12-06/entertainment/25854992_1_randy-blauvelt-father-flanagan-movie-lovers.

6. Charles Murray, "The Coming White Underclass," *Wall Street Journal*, October 29, 1993.

7. Richard O'Mara, "Are Orphanages Better for Kids than Welfare?" *Baltimore Sun*, November 27, 1994, http://articles.baltimoresun.com/1994-11-27/news/1994331010_1_orphanages-newt-gingrich-illegitimacy.

8. Joe Klein, *The Natural: The Misunderstood Presidency of Bill Clinton* (New York: Broadway Books, 2003), 155.

9. Peter Edelman, "The Worst Thing Bill Clinton Has Done," *Atlantic*, March 1997, www.theatlantic.com/magazine/archive/1997/03/the-worst-thing-bill-clinton-has-done/376797/.

10. Dorothy Roberts, *Shattered Bonds: The Color of Child Welfare* (New York: Basic Civitas, 2002), 108.

11. I am using "middle class" more as a cultural term than a description of economic position. In the United States, working-class people with relatively stable employment are encouraged to identify as middle class, especially if they own a home (even if heavily mortgaged), live in a two-parent household, and have the ability to save for retirement.

Chapter Two: Moving Toward a Racialized Child Welfare System

1. "Narrative of Sojourner Truth," 1850, http://digital.library.upenn.edu/women/truth/1850/1850.html#16.

2. Kate Larsen, *Bound for the Promised Land: Harriet Tubman; Portrait of an American Hero* (New York: Ballantine Books, 2004), 33, 89–90.

3. Truman Nelson, *The Old Man: John Brown at Harpers Ferry* (Chicago: Haymarket Books, 2009), 69–71.

4. W. E. B. Du Bois, "The Freedmen's Bureau," *Atlantic Monthly* 87 (1901): 354–65, 361.

5. Keeanga-Yamahtta Taylor, "Review: W. E. B. Du Bois: Black Reconstruction in America 1860–1880," *International Socialist Review* 57, January–February 2008.

6. Mary Niall Mitchell, *Raising Freedom's Child: Black Children and Visions of the Future after Slavery* (New York: NYU Press, 2008), Kindle ed., Loc. 1828.

7. Malcolm X with Alex Haley, *The Autobiography of Malcolm X* (New York: Ballantine Books, 1987), 10–21.

8. Manning Marable, *Malcolm X: A Life of Reinvention* (New York: Penguin Books, 2011), 35–37.

9. Martha Satz and Lori Askeland, "Civil Rights, Adoption Rights: Domestic Adoption and Foster Care, 1970 to the Present," in *Children and Youth in Orphanages, Adoption and Foster Care: A Historical Handbook and Guide*, Lori Askeland, ed. (Westport, CT: Greenwood Press, 2006), 53–55.

10. I find the NABSW position troubling, in part because I know many biracial homes in which good parenting occurs. Parenthetically, I am also the white (non-adoptive) stepparent of two Black children, and I like to think that on my good days I coparent competently. The 1972 document is persuasive in analyzing the impact of racism on Black children, and in pointing out that proponents of transracial adoption often seem to suggest that white parents are likely to be superior. NABSW was not wrong to suggest that kinship and community ties were devalued among advocates for adoption generally and transracial adoption specifically.

Nevertheless, I find the "vehement stance against placement of Black children in white homes for any reason" problematic because it suggests that the social construct of race is more powerful than the ability of parents and children to form families. Such placements raise complex issues that should be considered, but I oppose an absolute ban. This does not negate the fact that the call for "color-blind adoption" includes racist arguments of varying degrees of subtlety.

11. Elizabeth Bartholet, *Nobody's Children: Abuse, Neglect, Foster Drift and the Adoption Alternative* (New York: Beacon Press, 1999).

12. Ruth McCoy, "Expedited Permanency: Implications for African-American Children and Families," *Virginia Journal of Social Policy and the Law* 12 (2005): 477–81.

13. *Loving v. Virginia*, 388 U.S. 1 (1967) was a Supreme Court case striking down "anti-miscegenation laws" prohibiting interracial marriage. See also U.S. Commission on Civil Rights, "Minorities in Foster Care and Adoption: Briefing Report," 2010, 37.

14. "Haiti's Children and the Adoption Question," *Room for Debate*, *New York Times*, February 1, 2010, http://roomfordebate.blogs.nytimes.com/ 2010/02/01/haitis-children-and-the-adoption-question/.

15. See Hearings on H.R. 10032 before the House Committee on Ways and Means, 87th Cong., 2nd Sess., 294–97, 305, 307 (1962).

16. According to data from the NYC Administration for Children's Services, for example, in New York City in 2011, of the more than twenty thousand cases "indicated" (or substantiated after investigation by a Child Protective Specialist), 81 percent were indicated for neglect alone, 3 percent for abuse alone, and 15 percent for some combination of abuse and neglect.

17. Quoted in Judith Sealander, *The Failed Century of the Child: Governing America's Young in the Twentieth Century* (Cambridge: Cambridge University Press, 2003), 3.

18. Lee, *Catching a Case*, 150.

19. African American children were 14 percent of the total child population in 2008, but 31 percent of children in foster care. American Indian/ Alaskan Native children were 1 percent of total child population, but accounted for 2 percent of foster care placements. White children, on the other hand, were 56 percent of the child population, but accounted for 40 percent of foster care population, while Asian children were 4 percent of child population and 1 percent of those in care. Hispanic children were 22 percent of the child population and 20 percent of those in care. www.childwelfare.gov/pubs/issue_briefs/racial_disproportionality/ racialdisp1.cfm.

20. Children's Defense Fund, *State of the Child 2014* (Washington, DC: Children's Defense Fund, 2014), 22.

21. Roberts, *Shattered Bonds*, 200–201.

22. Ibid.; also see, Dorothy Roberts, "The Racial Geography of Child Welfare: Toward a New Research Paradigm," *Child Welfare* 87, no. 2 (2008): 125–48.

23. Education Law Center of Pennsylvania, "Educational Outcomes for Children and Youth in Foster and Out-of-Home Care," 2007.

24. National Education Association and National Association of School Psychologists, *Truth in Labeling: Disproportionality in Special Education* (Washington, DC: National Education Association, 2007), 8.

25. Ben Baeder, "Studies: Disproportionate Number of Black Children End Up in L.A. Foster Care," *Inland Valley Daily Bulletin*, March 23, 2013, www.dailybulletin.com/news/ci_22857170/studies-disproportionate-number-black-children-wind-up-l.

26. Ibid.

27. Sedlak, et al., "Fourth National Incidence Report on Child Abuse and Neglect: Report to Congress," 2.

28. Sedlak, McPherson, and Das, "Supplementary Analyses of Race Differences in Child Maltreatment Rates in the [NIS-4]," 1.

29. Dorothy Roberts, "Prison, Foster Care and the Systemic Punishment of Black Mothers," *UCLA Law Review* 59 (2012): 1474, 1488.

30. Eric Williams, *Capitalism and Slavery* (Chapel Hill: University of North Carolina Press, 1994), 7.

31. W. E. B. Du Bois, *Black Reconstruction in America 1860–1880* (New York: Free Press, 1935), 39.

32. Frederick Douglass, "Reply of the Colored Delegation to the President," 1866, University of Rochester, Frederick Douglass Project Writings, http://rbscp.lib.rochester.edu/4391.

33. Sharon Smith, *Subterranean Fire: A History of Working-Class Radicalism in the United States* (Chicago: Haymarket Books, 2006), 45.

34. Vincent Schilling, "Center for Native American Youth Addresses Foster Care 'Scandal,'" *Indian Country Today Media Network*, June 12, 2013, http://indiancountrytodaymedianetwork.com/2013/06/12/center-native-american-youth-addresses-foster-care-scandal-149846.

35. "An Apology: Remarks of Kevin Gover, Assistant Secretary–Indian Affairs, Department of the Interior at the Ceremony Acknowledging the 175th Anniversary of the Establishment of the Bureau of Indian Affairs," September 8, 2000, www.tahtonka.com/apology.html.

36. David Wallace Adams, *Educating for Extinction: American Indians and the Boarding School Experience, 1875–1928* (Lawrence: University Press of Kansas, 1995), 23.

37. Charla Bear, "American Indian Boarding Schools Haunt Many," National Public Radio, May 12, 2008, www.npr.org/templates/story/story.php?storyId=16516865.

38. National Indian Child Welfare Association, "Effective Leadership for Tribal Child Welfare," undated, www.nicwa.org/Indian_Child_Welfare

_Act/documents/2015%20Effective%20Leadership%20for%20 Tribal%20Child%20Welfare.pdf.

39. Martha Stoddard, "Rising Disparity Seen in Rate of Native American Kids in Foster Care," *Omaha.com*, November 15, 2013, www.omaha. com/news/rising-disparity-seen-in-rate-of-native-american-kids-in/ article_ac1bcdc5-912a-5f8e-9faf-def64e8786c2.html.

40. Adoptive Couple v. Baby Girl, Slip Op. No. 12-399 at 16 (U.S. 2013).

41. Dan Frosch, "Focus on Preserving Heritage Can Limit Foster Care for Indians," *New York Times*, January 26, 2013, www.nytimes.com/2013/01/27/ us/focus-on-heritage-hinders-foster-care-for-indians.html.

42. National Indian Child Welfare Association, "Dr. Phil Show Fact Check," www.nicwa.org/babyveronica/documents/DrPhilICWAFactCheck. pdf.

Chapter Three: Parents with Disabilities

1. "Annual Disability Statistics Compendium," Table 3.11, Institute on Disability, University of New Hampshire, http://disabilitycompendium. org/statistics/poverty.

2. Ibid., Table 2.9.

3. Ibid., Table 4.1.

4. *Rocking the Cradle: Ensuring the Rights of Parents with Disabilities and Their Children* (Washington, DC: National Council on Disability, 2012), 17.

5. Michael Oliver and Colin Barnes, *The New Politics of Disablement* (New York: Palgrave Macmillan, 2012), 6.

6. Ibid., 3.

7. Victor Finkelstein, *Attitudes and Disabled People*, World Rehabilitation Fund Monograph No. 5, 1980, http://disability-studies.leeds.ac.uk/library /author/finkelstein.vic.

8. See, generally, James W. Trent, Jr., *Inventing the Feeble Mind: A History of Mental Retardation in the United States* (Berkeley and Los Angeles: University of California Press, 1994).

9. The ensuing discussion of eugenics is based on the following sources: Trent, *Inventing the Feeble Mind*; Randall Hansen and Desmond King, *Sterilized by the State: Eugenics, Race and the Population Scare in Twentieth-Century North America* (New York: Cambridge University Press, 2013); Edwin Black, *War Against the Weak: Eugenics and America's Campaign to Create a Master Race* (Chicago: Dialog Press, 2012); Paul A. Lombardo, ed., *A Century of Eugenics: From the Indiana Experiment to the Human Genome Era* (Bloomington: Indiana University Press, 2011); Wendy Kline, "Eugenics in the United States," in *The Oxford Handbook of the History of Eugenics*, Alison Bashford and Philippa Levine, eds. (New York: Oxford University Press, 2010).

10. Buck v. Bell, 274 US 200 (1927).

11. "Investigative Report Regarding the 'Ashley Treatment,'" Washington Protection and Advocacy System, 2007.
12. National Council on Disability, *Rocking the Cradle*, 45.
13. *Guardianship of Mary Moe*, 81 Mass. App. Ct. 136 (2012).
14. National Council on Disability, *Rocking the Cradle*, 45.
15. Katharine M. Hill, Elizabeth Lightfoot, and Traci LaLiberte, "The Inclusion of Disability as a Condition for Termination of Parental Rights," *Child Abuse and Neglect* 34 (2010): 931.
16. The vignette following this chapter concerns a parent with autism who was "fast-tracked" for TPR.
17. Letter of Findings, Investigation of the Massachusetts Department of Children and Families by the United States Departments of Justice and Health and Human Services Pursuant to the Americans with Disabilities Act and the Rehabilitation Act (DJ No. 204-36-216 and HHS No. 14-182176), 12, www.hhs.gov/sites/default/files/mass_lof.pdf.
18. Megan Kirshbaum, "A Brief History of Through the Looking Glass," Through the Looking Glass, www.lookingglass.org/who-we-are/history.
19. Kim E. Nielsen, *A Disability History of the United State* (Boston: Beacon Press, 2012), 162–63.
20. Oliver and Barnes, *New Politics of Disablement*, 136–37.

Chapter Four: Foster Youth

1. This chapter focuses briefly on how the structure of the foster care system may perpetuate harm and create the risk of future harm to foster children. It is not intended as an indictment of foster parents or the people who work with foster youth. It presents the perspectives of some foster youth on their experiences, sometimes using language condemning workers and foster parents they have encountered. The aim is not to suggest that these quotes accurately describe most foster parents and workers, but rather to provide evidence of the effect of the current system on the youth for whose benefit it was ostensibly created, and to argue for its fundamental transformation.
2. Malika Saada Saar, "Stopping the Foster Care to Child Trafficking Pipeline," *Huffington Post*, October 29, 2013, www.huffingtonpost.com/malika-saada-saar/stopping-the-foster-care-_b_4170483.html.
3. Ibid.
4. Delilah Bruskas and Dale H. Tessin, "Adverse Childhood Experiences and Psychosocial Well-Being of Women Who Were in Foster Care as Children," *Permenente Journal* 17, no. 3 (Summer 2013): e132, www.ncbi.nlm.nih.gov/pmc/articles/PMC3783064/pdf/permj17_3pe131.pdf.
5. Julian Dominguez and Melinda Murphy, *A Culture of Fear: An Inside Look at Los Angeles County's Department of Children and Family Services* (Houston: Strategic Books, 2014), 30.

6. Matthew D. Bramlett and Laura F. Radel, "Adverse Family Experiences Among Children in Nonparental Care, 2011–2012," National Health Statistics Report No. 74, May 7, 2014.

7. Bruskas and Tessin, "Adverse Childhood Experiences," 136.

8. "Tales of Foster Care Abuse Sound Like Prison," Associated Press, July 24, 2013, http://kxan.com/2014/07/24/house-committee-scrutinizing-texas-foster-care/.

9. Reuven Blau, "Alleged Long Island Pedophile Was Investigated Nine Times since 1998 for Abusing Foster Kids, but Authorities Did Nothing," *New York Daily News*, March 28, 2016, www.nydailynews.com/new-york/pedophile-probed-9-times-abusing-foster-kids-article-1.2579573; Carol Potsky, "LI Foster Home Sexual Abuse Case Prompts Inspections by NYC," *Newsday*, April 11, 2016, www.newsday.com/long-island/li-foster-home-sexual-abuse-case-prompts-inspections-by-nyc-1.11666569.

10. Paulo Freire, *Pedagogy of the Oppressed* (New York: Continuum International Publishing Group, 2000), 89.

11. "Foster Children: HHS Guidance Could Help States Improve Oversight of Psychotropic Prescriptions," (Washington, DC: U.S. General Accountability Office, 2011), GAO-12-270T.

12. "Foster Care," Child Trends Databank, 2014, www.childtrends.org/?indicators=foster-care.

13. "Midwest Evaluation of the Adult Functioning of Former Foster Youth," Chapin Hall at the University of Chicago, 2011, www.chapinhall.org/sites/default/files/Midwest%20Evaluation_Report_4_10_12.pdf.

14. "Pregnant and Parenting Teens in Foster Care: Prevention Efforts and Supportive Services to Meet the Needs of Youth in Care" (New York: National Resource Center for Permanency and Family Connections, 2013), 4.

15. "Fostering Success in Education: National Factsheet on the Educational Outcomes of Children in Foster Care," American Bar Association, Center for Foster Care and Education, January 2014.

16. Sherry Wolf, "The Roots of Gay Oppression," *International Socialist Review* 37, September–October 2004.

17. David Tobis, *From Pariahs to Partners: How Parents and Their Allies Changed New York City's Child Welfare System*, (New York: Oxford University Press, 2013), Kindle ed., Loc. 601–24.

18. Priya Sikerwar and Erin Rider, "Transgender Youth in Child Welfare Settings," National Center for Child Welfare Excellence at Silberman School for Social Work, 2015, www.nccwe.org/downloads/info-packs/Rider.Sikerwar.pdf.

Chapter Five: Foster Parents

1. "Six Kids Neglected by Florida Foster Care," *20/20*, May 24, 2002, http://abcnews.go.com/2020/story?id=123897&page=1.

2. Review by the author of 2009 Forms 990 (tax-exempt organization information returns) filed with the Internal Revenue Service, accessed at http://irs990.charityblossom.org. A small number of agencies did not have Forms 990 online, but the agencies reviewed account for the overwhelming majority of foster care placements in New York City.

3. Some foster parents, particularly "house parents" in congregate care settings, do receive wages in addition to board payment. They may also live in housing provided by the public or nonprofit agency.

4. William P. O'Hare, "Data on Children in Foster Care from the Census Bureau," KidsCount/Ann E. Casey Foundation, June 2008, 20, 26.

5. "Raising Servants of Christ," http://raisingservantsofchrist.com. Quotation retrieved from http://about.me/dkbaltodano.

6. South Carolina Code of Laws, section 59-65-46.

7. Megan Twohey, "The Child Exchange: Inside America's Underground Market for Adopted Children," Reuters Investigates, September 9–11, 2013, www.reuters.com/investigates/adoption/#article/part1.

8. Benjamin Hardy, "A Child Left Unprotected," *Arkansas Times*, March 5, 2015, 1.

9. Jen Hayden, "Arkansas Rep. Justin Harris Gave His Adopted Children Away to a Man Who Raped One of Them," *Daily Kos*, March 5, 2015, www.dailykos.com/story/2015/03/05/1368833/-Arkansas-Rep-Justin-Harris-gave-his-adopted-children-away-to-a-man-who-raped-one-of-them.

Chapter Six: Juvenile "Justice"

1. David Tanenhaus, "Justice for the Child: The Beginning of the Juvenile Court in Chicago," *Chicago History* 24, no. 2 (Winter 1998): 8.

2. Judith Sealander, *The Failed Century of the Child: Governing America's Young in the Twentieth Century* (New York: Cambridge University Press, 2003), 21.

3. In re Gault, 387 U.S. 1 (1967).

4. In re Winship, 397 U.S. 358 (1970).

5. *Juvenile Offenders and Victims: 2006 National Report* (U.S. Department of Justice, Office of Juvenile Justice and Delinquency Prevention, 2006), 200.

6. *Justice on Trial: Racial Disparities in the American Criminal Justice System* (Leadership Conference on Civil Rights, 2000), ch. 5, "Race and the Juvenile Justice System."

7. Sealander, *Failed Century of the Child*, 50–51.

8. *Juvenile Offenders and Victims*, 202.

9. William Ecanbarger, *Kids for Cash: Two Judges, Thousands of Children and a $2.8 Million Kickback Scheme* (New York: New Press, 2012).
10. Ibid., 254–55.
11. Ibid., 97.
12. USA v. City of Meridian, Case 4:12-cv-00168-HTW-LRA, Complaint, October 24, 2012, U.S. District Court, SD Mississippi, www.justice.gov /crt/about/spl/documents/meridian_complaint_10-24-12.pdf.
13. Office of Juvenile Justice and Delinquency Prevention, "Juvenile Suicide in Confinement: A National Survey," 2009, U.S. Justice Department, viii.
14. Kelly Davis, "Legislation Seeks to End Isolation in Juvenile Facilities," *San Diego City Beat*, February 5, 2015, www.sdcitybeat.com/sandiego /article-13869-legislation-seeks-to-end-isolation-in-juvenile-facilities .html.
15. D.C. Herz, J. P. Ryan, and S. Bilchik, "Challenges Facing Crossover Youth: An Examination of Juvenile-Justice Decision Making and Recidivism," *Family Court Review* 48, no. 2 (April 2010): 305–21.
16. "Facts on Foster Care in America," ABC News, May 30, 2006, http:// abcnews.go.com/Primetime/FosterCare/story?id=2017991&page=1.
17. Tobis, *From Pariahs to Partners*, Kindle ed., Loc. 2984.
18. Roberts, "Prison, Foster Care, and the Systemic Punishment of Black Mothers," 1477–78.
19. "Balanced and Restorative Justice for Juveniles: A Framework for Juvenile Justice in the 21st Century," (University of Minnesota and Florida Atlantic University, Office of Juvenile Justice and Delinquency Prevention, 1997), www.ncjrs.gov/pdffiles/framwork.pdf.

Chapter Seven: Toiling Inside the Bureaucracy

1. Michael Lipsky, "Toward a Theory of Street-Level Bureaucracy," Institute for Research on Poverty, University of Wisconsin, 1969, 2, www.historyofsocialwork.org.
2. Julian Dominguez and Melinda Murphy, *A Culture of Fear: An Inside Look at Los Angeles County's Department of Children and Family Services* (Houston: Strategic Books, 2014), 38.
3. Walter I. Trattner, *From Poor Law to Welfare State: A History of Social Welfare in America* (New York: Free Press, 1999), 94.
4. Ibid., 95.
5. Mary Ellen Richmond, *The Good Neighbor in the City* (Philadelphia: J. B. Lippincott Co., 1908), 42.
6. Ibid., 97–98.
7. Michael Reisch and Janice Andrews, *The Road Not Taken: A History of Radical Social Work in the United States* (New York: Routledge, 2012), 29–30.
8. Ibid., 61–85.

9. Ibid., 95–97; Mark H. Maier, *City Unions: Managing Discontent in New York City* (New Brunswick, NJ: Rutgers University Press, 1987), 57–58.
10. Maier, *City Unions*, 69–72.
11. Frances Fox Piven and Richard Cloward, "Notes Toward a Radical Social Work," in *Radical Social Work*, Roy Bailey and Mike Brake, eds. (New York: Pantheon Books, 1976), xxii–xxviii.
12. Reisch and Andrews, *The Road Not Taken*, 200, 208.
13. National Association of Social Workers (NASW), "Institutional Racism and the Social Work Profession: A Call to Action," 2007, www.naswdc.org/diversity/InstitutionalRacism.pdf.
14. NASW, "Code of Ethics," www.socialworkers.org/pubs/code/code.asp.
15. Roy Bailey and Mike Brake, "Appendix: Case Con Manifesto," in *Radical Social Work*, 146–47.
16. Kevin Flynn et al., "Child Welfare Unit in Crisis, Cuts in Budget, Staff Take a Toll," *New York Daily News*, December 3, 1995, www.nydailynews.com/archives/news/child-welfare-unit-crisis-cuts-budget-staff-toll-article-1.697417.
17. Richard Steier, *Enough Blame to Go Around: The Labor Pains of New York City's Public Employee Unions*, (Albany: State University of New York Press, 2014).
18. Richard Wexler, "Foster Care Panic in Los Angeles," National Coalition for Child Protection Reform, www.nccpr.org/reports/LA2010.pdf.
19. The preceding passage relies on ibid.; Garrett Theiroff, "Private Foster Care System, Intended to Save Children, Endangers Some," Los Angeles Times, December 18, 2013, http://www.latimes.com/local/la-me-foster-care-dto-htmlstory.html.
20. Don Lash, "Social Workers Win a Victory," *Socialist Worker*, March 17, 2014, http://socialistworker.org/2014/03/17/social-workers-win-a-victory.
21. Lassiter v. Department of Soc. Servs., 452 U.S. 18 (1981).
22. Astra Outley, "Representation for Children and Families in Dependency Proceedings," Pew Charitable Trust, Commission on Children in Foster Care, 2009, www.pewtrusts.org/en/archived-projects/commission-on-children-in-foster-care.
23. See the National Lawyers' Guild website: www.nlg.org.

Chapter Eight: The Future of Child Welfare?

1. Children's Bureau, Administration for Children and Families, "Trends in Foster Care and Adoption: FFY 2002–FFY 2013," (2014), U.S. Department of Health and Human Services.
2. Tobis, *From Pariahs to Partners*, Kindle ed., Loc. 3695.
3. National Conference of State Legislatures, "Legislative Strategies to Safely Reduce the Number of Children in Foster Care," 2010, Table 1, p. 2.

4. Richard Wexler, "Foster Care Panic in Los Angeles," National Coalition for Child Protection Reform, 2011, 13.
5. Todd Reed, "Crack Baby Myth Goes Up in Smoke," *Al Jazeera America*, March 8, 2015, http://america.aljazeera.com/watch/shows/america-tonight/articles/2015/3/10/crack-baby-myth.html.
6. Roberts, *Killing the Black Body*, 19–20.
7. National Coalition for Child Protection Reform (NCCPR), "Foster Care Panics: Issue Paper No. 2," 2011.
8. National Coalition for Child Protection Reform, "Why Foster Care Panics Don't Happen in Reverse," NCCPR blog, 2006, www.nccprblog.org/2006/10/why-foster-care-panics-dont-work-in.html.
9. Ginger Adams Otis et al., "Battle Brews over Body of Starved, Tortured 4-Year-Old Myls Dobson, Killed While under Care of Baby-Sitter," January 14, 2014, *New York Daily News*, www.nydailynews.com/new-york/nyc-crime/body-myls-dobson-remains-unclaimed-article-1.1579293.
10. Andrew White, "The Dream of Reinvestment," *Child Welfare Watch* 21 (Winter 2011–2012): 5–6.
11. Erwin A. Blackstone et al., "Privatizing Adoption and Foster Care: Applying Auction and Market Solutions," *Children and Youth Services Review* 26 (2004): 1033–1049.
12. Roland Zullo, "Child Welfare Privatization and Child Welfare: Can the Two Be Efficiently Reconciled?" Center for Labor Studies, University of Michigan, undated, http://irlee.umich.edu/Publications/Docs/ChildWelfarePrivatization.pdf.
13. Aram Roston, "'Culture of Incompetence': For-Profit Foster-Care Giant Is Leaving Illinois," *BuzzFeed News*, April 17, 2015, www.buzzfeed.com/aramroston/mentorleavesillinois#.wk6DDrv6W.
14. Sally Kestin, "Salaries for Florida's Child Care Officials Are Out of Control, Lawmakers Say," *Sun-Sentinel*, April 2, 2011, http://articles.sun-sentinel.com/2011-04-02/news/fl-child-welfare-privatization-20110401_1_child-welfare-salaries-ceo-emilio-benitez.
15. Brian Peacock, "Interim Evaluation of Florida's Child Welfare Privatization Project," Florida Department of Children and Families, March 1998, viii, www.dcf.state.fl.us/admin/publications/docs/chldwel1.doc.
16. Kevin O'Hanlon, "Privatization Fails: Nebraska Tries Again to Reform Child Welfare," Center for Public Integrity, August 21, 2012, www.publicintegrity.org/2012/08/21/10706/privatization-fails-nebraska-tries-again-reform-child-welfare.
17. Beth Cortez-Neavel, "State Stumbles Forward with Foster Care Privatization," *Texas Observer*, September 9, 2014, www.texasobserver.org/experiment-partially-privatizing-foster-care-failure.
18. Carol Marbin Miller, "Misconduct Found at Privately Run Child-Welfare Agency," March 17, 2015, *Miami Herald*, www.miamiherald.com/news/local/community/broward/article15197171.html.

Chapter Nine: Real Reform

1. Carlos Nelson Coutinho, *Gramsci's Political Thought* (Chicago: Haymarket Books, 2013), 81.
2. Ibid., 83.
3. Bob Mulally, *Structural Social Work: Ideology, Theory and Practice*, 2nd ed. (Ontario: Oxford University Press, 1997), 19.
4. "Gov. Gregoire Delivers Keynote Speech at Children's Justice Conference," transcript, 2006, https://www.highbeam.com/doc/1P3-1062470371 .html.
5. Shay Bilchik, "Producing High-Quality Advocacy for Children and Families," Keynote Address, National Association of Council for Children National Children's Law Conference, 2004, http://66.227 .70.18/execdir/edremarks040907.htm.
6. Sealander, *Failed Century of the Child*, 21.
7. "From Rights to Reality: A Plan for Parent Advocacy and Family-Centered Child Welfare Reform," *Rise*, 2011, www.risemagazine.org /PDF/From_Rights_to_Reality.pdf.
8. "DHS/DCFS Give Us Back Our Children," Global Women's Strike, www.globalwomenstrike.net/content/dhsdcfs-give-us-back-our-children.
9. In fairness, Mullaly wrote that before the Social Democrats relinquished power and Sweden began moving toward the neoliberal consensus in Europe.
10. Sven Hessle and Bo Vinnerljung, "Child Welfare in Sweden: An Overview," rev. ed., Stockholm University, Department of Social Work, working paper, 2000, www.sws.soton.ac.uk/cwab/Guide/KRsweden.doc.
11. Ibid.
12. Ibid.
13. Mattias Tyden, "The Scandinavian States: Reform Eugenics Applied," and Véronique Mottier, "Eugenics and the State: Policy Making in Comparative Perspective," *The Oxford Handbook of the History of Eugenics* (New York: Oxford University Press, 2010), 134–53, 363–76.
14. Judith Orr, "Z Is for Zhenotdel," *Socialist Review*, September 2009, www.socialistreview.org.uk/article.php?articlenumber=10938.
15. Minnesota State Bar Association, "Cuba's Legal Composite: A Blend of the Familiar and the Foreign," *Bench & Bar of Minnesota*, January 11, 2012.
16. Friedrich Engels, *Anti-Dühring*, 1877, part 3, ch. 2, Marxists Internet Archive, www.marxists.org/archive/marx/works/1877/anti-duhring/ch24 .htm.

Chapter Ten: Child Welfare and Social Reproduction

1. Although this is true in theory, some employers have managed to develop a business model that allows them to pay less than a living wage for workers with families by taking advantage of the minimal welfare provisions available to supplement wages. Thus, there are accounts of

Walmart human resources personnel who help employees apply for food stamps and Medicaid. These programs are in effect subsidizing the employer, which recognizes the need to provide for social reproduction, but is able to use public money to do it. This is not a contradiction of social reproduction theory but entirely consistent. See Alex Callinicos, *The Revolutionary Ideas of Karl Marx* (Chicago: Haymarket Books, 2011), 131.

2. Lise Vogel, *Marxism and the Oppression of Women* (Chicago: Haymarket Books, 2013), 60.

3. Karl Marx, *Capital*, 1867, vol. 1, ch. 6, Marxists Internet Archive, www.marxists.org/archive/marx/works/1867-c1/ch06.htm.

4. Friedrich Engels, *Origins of the Family, Private Property, and the State*, "The Monogamous Family," part II, ch. 4, Marxists Internet Archive, www.marxists.org/archive/marx/works/1884/origin-family/ch02d.htm.

5. Sharon Smith, "Engels and the Origin of Women's Oppression," *International Socialist Review*, no. 2 (Fall 1997), www.isreview.org/issues/02/engles_family.shtml.

6. Vogel, *Marxism and the Oppression of Women*, 61.

7. Ibid., 71.

8. Drew Desilver, "Black Unemployment Rate Is Consistently Twice That of Whites," Pew Research Center, August 21, 2013, www.pewresearch.org/fact-tank/2013/08/21/through-good-times-and-bad-black-unemployment-is-consistently-double-that-of-whites/.

9. Katherine Peralta, "Native Americans Left Behind in the Economic Recovery," *U.S. News and World Report*, November 27, 2014, www.usnews.com/news/articles/2014/11/27/native-americans-left-behind-in-the-economic-recovery.

10. Jens Manuel Krogstad, "Hispanics Only Group to See Its Poverty Rate Decline and Incomes Rise," FactTank, Pew Research Center, September 19, 2014, www.pewresearch.org/fact-tank/2014/09/19/hispanics-only-group-to-see-its-poverty-rate-decline-and-incomes-rise/.

11. "Among Wealthy Nations, US Stands Alone in Its Embrace of Religion," Pew Global Studies, December 10, 2002, www.pewglobal.org/2002/12/19/among-wealthy-nations/.

12. U.S. State Department, "International Religious Freedom Report 2004–Finland," www.state.gov/j/drl/rls/irf/2004/35453.htm; European Commission, "Eurobarometer Report: Biotechnology," October 2010, http://ec.europa.eu/public_opinion/archives/ebs/ebs_341_en.pdf.

13. "Transcript: Dr. Bill Cosby Speaks at the 50th Anniversary Commemoration of the Brown vs. Topeka Board of Education, Supreme Court Decision," www.rci.rutgers.edu/~schochet/101/Cosby_Speech.htm.

14. See, generally, Edwin Black, *War Against the Weak: Eugenics and America's Campaign to Create a Master Race* (Washington, DC: Dialog Press, 2012).

Chapter Eleven: Socialism and the Parent-Child Relationship

1. Karl Marx and Friedrich Engels, *Theses on Feuerbach*, 1845, Marxists Internet Archive, www.marxists.org/archive/marx/works/1845/theses /theses.htm.
2. Karl Marx and Friedrich Engels, *The German Ideology*, 1845, Marxists Internet Archive, www.marxists.org/archive/marx/works/1845/german -ideology/.
3. Friedrich Engels, *Principles of Communism*, 1847, Marxists Internet Archive, www.marxists.org/archive/marx/works/1847/11/prin-com.htm.
4. Karl Marx and Friedrich Engels, *The Communist Manifesto* (Chicago: Haymarket Books, 2005), 64–65.
5. Heather A. Brown, *Marx on Gender and the Family: A Critical Study* (Chicago: Haymarket Books, 2013), 58.
6. Karl Marx, *Capital*, vol. 1 (New York: Penguin Books, 1976), 621.
7. Karl Marx, *1844 Philosophical and Economic Manuscripts*, 1st Manuscript: "Estranged Labour," Marxists Internet Archive, www.marxists.org /archive/marx/works/1844/manuscripts/preface.htm.
8. Ibid.
9. Karl Marx, 3rd Manuscript: "Private Property and Communism," Marxists Internet Archive, www.marxists.org/archive/marx/works/1844 /manuscripts/comm.htm.
10. Engels, *Origin of the Family*, ch. 2.
11. Cathy Porter, *Alexandra Kollontai* (Chicago: Haymarket Books, 2014), 304.
12. Alexandra Kollontai, *Communism and the Family* (1920), Marxists Internet Archive, www.marxists.org/archive/kollonta/1920/communism-family .htm.
13. Ibid.
14. Ibid.
15. Pavel A. Parfentiev, "A Brief History of Family Policy in Russia, 1917– 2013," *The Family in America* 27, no. 3 (Summer 2013): 237.
16. Reisch and Andrews, *The Road Not Taken*, 49.
17. Congressional Record—Appendix, January 10, 1963, A34–A35.
18. Porter, *Alexandra Kollontai*, 424.

Index

"Passim" (literally "scattered") indicates intermittent discussion of a topic over a cluster of pages.

abandoned children, 9, 107, 165
abortion, 186; involuntary, 68, 69
addiction. *See* drug abuse/addiction
Administration for Children's Services (ACS). *See* New York City, Administration for Children's Services (ACS)
adoption, 35, 37, 44–45, 69, 101, 175; "auction model," 148–49; of child detainees, 107; by Christian missionaries, 104; LGBTQ, 86; Native Americans, 53; youth views, 90. *See also* international adoption; transracial adoption
Adoption and Safe Families Act (ASFA) of 1997, 25, 44, 49, 69–70, 174–75
Adoption Assistance and Child Welfare Act, 44
Adoptive Couple v. Baby Girl. See Baby Veronica case
AFDC. *See* Aid to Families with Dependent Children (AFDC)
African Americans, 10–11, 25, 31–52 passim, 159, 187, 198n19; in criminal justice system, 45–46; in juvenile justice system, 109–10; mothers, 2, 124; in religion-based foster care, 105, 136; school arrests, 112; transracial adoption, 40, 197–98n10; unemployment, 173
African American Social Workers. *See* National Association of Black Social Workers (NABSW)
AFSCME. *See* American Federation of State, County, and Municipal Employees (AFSCME)
"aging out." *See* foster care: aging out
AIDS. *See* HIV/AIDS
Aid to Families with Dependent Children (AFDC), 38–39, 42, 124, 129
Alaska, 52, 102
alcohol abuse (alcoholism), 7, 9, 34, 49, 65, 163. *See also* drunk driving
alcohol drinking. *See* drinking
alienation, 182
Ali Forney Center, New York City, 96
Alliance Human Services, 149
All Kids, 150
American Federation of State, County, and Municipal Employees (AFSCME), 131
American Indian Policy Review Commission, 56
American Indians. *See* Native Americans
anger, 26, 27, 28, 43, 82
animal functions, humans', 182
Ann E. Casey Foundation. *See* Casey Foundation

anticommunism, 122–23, 130, 186
Arkansas, 86
ASFA. *See* Adoption and Safe Families Act (ASFA) of 1997
"Ashley Treatment," 68
Asian American children, 45, 198n19
asylums and custodial hospitals, 39, 62, 63, 67
atheism, 175
attorney. *See* lawyers
"auction model" for adoption. *See* adoption: "auction model"
August Aichhorn Center for Adolescent Residential Care, 93–97 passim
austerity measures, 10, 127, 129
autism, 75

babies, newborn. *See* newborns
Baby Veronica case, 53–54
background checks. *See* criminal background checks
backlash, racist, 40, 42, 43, 46
Bailey, Ray: *Radical Social Work*: 125–27, 130
Baltimore, 110
Barnes, Colin, 61
Bartholet, Elizabeth, 40, 41, 48–49
Bennett, William, 23, 157
Berkeley, California, 73
Bilchik, Shay, 158
Black Americans. *See* African Americans
Black Codes, 33
blaming the victim, 25, 44, 120, 126, 156, 157, 174
Bloomberg, Michael, 1
boarding schools, 23, 52, 55
Bolshevik Revolution. *See* Russian Revolution
Boys Town (film), 23
Brace, Charles Loring, 8, 19–20, 119; *The Life of the Street Rats*, 20

Brake, Mike, *Radical Social Work*: 125–27, 130
Braun, Carol Moseley, 41
Bread and Roses Strike (1912), 21–22
"breaking the cycle" (phrase), 12–13, 84
bribery, 111–13 passim
Britain. *See* Great Britain
Bronx Defenders, 137, 138
Brown, Heather, 181
Browning, Philip, 134
Buck. v. Bell, 65–66
Bureau of Indian Affairs (BIA), 52–53, 55, 56
Bush, George H. W., 144

California, 56, 66, 73–76 passim, 110–11
Capital (Marx), 182
capitalism, 8–12 passim, 50–52, 86, 114–15, 154–59 passim, 165–77 passim, 181–83 passim
capitation payment, 151
Casey Foundation, 158–59
Catalyst Collective, 128
Catholic Guardian Society and Home Bureau, 95
Catholic organizations, 21, 87, 95, 104–5
Catholics, 20, 21, 66
Center for Family Representation (CFR), 137, 138
CEO salaries. *See* executive income
charity, "scientific." *See* "scientific charity"
Charity Organizing Society (COS), 120
chemical dependency. *See* alcohol abuse (alcoholism); drug abuse/addiction
Chicago, 45, 108, 132, 144
child abuse, 43, 79–81 passim, 100, 147; media coverage, 132–33;

Myls Dobson case, 145–46; neglect conflated with, 154

Child Abuse Prevention and Treatment Act (CAPTA), 43, 135

childcare, 6, 10, 44, 79, 187; foster parent requirements, 103; Soviet Union, 164, 184

child labor, 22, 121, 180, 181

child maltreatment, 5, 9, 40, 43, 47–49 passim, 79, 154, 156, 159. See also child abuse

child neglect, 1–10 passim, 99, 143, 144, 154, 198n16; Bartholet, 48; children's courts and, 108; conflated with maltreatment, 43; disability and, 69; domestic violence and, 137; dominant paradigm, 157; by foster parents, 100; poverty and, 59; so-called, 22, 56. See also National Incident Study of Abuse and Neglect (NIS)

ChildNet, 151

child poverty, 45; US world rank, 9, 175

child protection specialists (CPSs), New York City, 1–3 passim

children, commodification of, 78, 79, 149, 152

children, death of, 79–80, 81, 131, 133, 145, 146. See also suicide

children of immigrants, 20, 22–23, 65, 163

Children's Aid Society, 19, 21, 100, 147

children's courts. See juvenile courts

Children's Exodus (Lawrence, Massachusetts), 21–22, 164

Children's Justice Conference, 158

child safety, 4, 132–34 passim, 144–49 passim, 158, 165, 166

child sex trafficking, 77–78

ChildStat (New York City), 1–3

Child Welfare League of America (CWLA), 53, 56

Child Welfare Organizing Project (CWOP), 160–62

child welfare professionals, 117–41

Christianity, 103, 104, 175. See also Catholics

CIO. See Congress of Industrial Organizations (CIO)

"civil society" (Gramsci), 12, 153, 154, 155, 157, 169

class action litigation, 105, 136–37

Clinton, Bill, 24, 25, 129, 144

Cloward, Richard, 125–27

cocaine, crack. See crack cocaine

"coercive state" (Gramsci), 12, 153–56 passim, 177

cognitive disabilities. See intellectual disabilities

Cold Spring Harbor, New York, 64, 67

college attendance, 84, 85, 96

ColorLines, 162

commodification of children. See children, commodification of

Communism and the Family (Kollontai), 184–86 passim

Communist Party, 122, 123; USSR, 184

"compliance" and "noncompliance," parental, 35, 44, 69, 154

compulsory sterilization. See sterilization: involuntary

conflict of interest, 126

congregate care. See foster care group homes

congressional hearings. See U.S. Congress: hearings

Congress of Industrial Organizations (CIO), 123, 130

Connecticut, 77

corporal punishment, 26, 27

corruption, 111–13, 131, 152

Cosby, Bill, 176

counter-hegemonic narratives, 155–57

court orders, 39, 68, 140

courts, juvenile. *See* juvenile courts
crack cocaine, 34, 144
criminal background checks, 38,
    102–3
criminal justice system, 4, 45–46,
    162; aged-out people in, 84;
    foster parents' history in, 102–3.
    See also drug arrests and con-
    victions; juvenile justice system;
    sentencing
"crossover youth," 113–15
Crumpton, Kamaal Dashiem, 88–92
Cuba, 165
Cuomo, Andrew, 129
curfews, 89, 93, 94, 96–97
custodial hospitals. *See* asylums and
    custodial hospitals
CWLA. *See* Child Welfare League
    of America (CWLA)
CWOP. *See* Child Welfare Orga-
    nizing Project (CWOP)

Darwin, Charles, 84
data-driven management, 1, 118
Davenport, Charles, 64
death of children. *See* children,
    death of
"delinquency" and "delinquent
    youth," 107, 108, 109
Democratic Party, 24, 128–29, 130,
    131
Department of Health and Human
    Services. *See* US Department of
    Health and Human Services
Department of Justice. *See* US
    Department of Justice
deportation, 23, 115, 162
Depression. *See* Great Depression
"deserving poor" and "undeserving
    poor," 21, 34–35
detention centers, for-profit. *See* for-
    profit detention centers
developmental disabilities. *See* intel-
    lectual disabilities

DHS/DCFS Give Us Back Our
    Children, 161
*Diagnostic and Statistical Manual of
    Mental Disorders* (DSM), 81–82
disability, 59–76, 128, 177; "social
    model," 60. *See also* intellectual
    disabilities; physical disabilities
divorce, 175, 186
Dr. Phil Show, 54
Dobson, Myls, 145–46
domestic violence, 7, 44, 48, 70, 125,
    137, 159
The Door (drop-in center), 96, 97
Douglass, Frederick, 51
drinking: as "status offense," 109. *See
    also* alcohol abuse (alcoholism);
    drunk driving
drop-in centers, 96, 97
drug abuse/addiction, 7, 10, 34, 35,
    40, 44, 49, 144; criminalization,
    79, 144; Sweden, 163; treatment
    services, 36, 43, 79, 146
drug arrests and convictions, 41,
    102–3, 110
Drug Offenders Sentencing Alter-
    natives, 35
drugs, prescription. *See* prescription
    drugs
drug war. *See* war on drugs
drunk driving, 102
DSM. See *Diagnostic and Statisti-
    cal Manual of Mental Disorders*
    (DSM)
Du Bois, W. E. B., 50

Edelman, Marion Wright, 43
Edelman, Peter, 24–25
education: disability and, 60–61;
    foster parent requirements, 103;
    homeschooling, 104; Soviet
    Union, 185. *See also* college
    attendance; GED programs;
    public education; schools
emergency housing, 96, 97

Engels, Friedrich, 8, 166, 171–72, 179–83 passim
ethics codes, professional, 129–30
eugenics, 23, 63–71, 144, 176–77; Sweden, 163–64
"evidence-based models," 195n1
exchange value, 170, 182
executive income, 100, 150
"extended theory of the state" (Gramsci), 153

faith-based foster care. See religion-based foster care
family, patriarchal and nuclear, 171–72, 174, 179–87
family violence. See domestic violence
fatalities, child. See children, death of
federal funding, 58, 85
"feeble-minded" (label), 62, 65, 164, 176
"feeble-minded," institutionalization of, 62–63, 65–66
fighting, 93, 110
Finkelstein, Victor, 61
Finns and Finland, 163, 175
Flemming, Arthur ("Flemming Rule"), 42
Florida, 83, 100, 115, 145, 150–51, 186
food stamps, 208n1
forced sterilization. See sterilization: involuntary
for-profit detention centers, 111–12
foster care, 4–5, 31, 77–97; African Americans, 10–11, 33, 36–37, 46–47, 198n19; aging out, 83, 84–86; alumni, 46; child abuse, 79–81 passim; children of addicts, 35; children of prisoners, 45; curfews, 89, 93, 94, 96–97; diagnostic labels in, 81–82; "drift," 40, 44; government spending, 7, 58; homeless youth,
93–97; LGBTQ youth, 86–87, 93–97; medication in, 83–84, 93; mentally ill youth, 93–97; Native Americans, 37, 52, 56, 57, 198n19; panics, 132–33, 145–47; population decline, 143; racial demographic, 198n19; "rate of removal," 132; religion-based, 21, 87, 103–5, 136–37; sex trafficking and, 77–78. See also "kinship" foster care
foster care group homes, 5, 24, 75, 88
Fostering Positive Action (FPA) Foundation, 160–61
foster parents, 99–105; abuse by, 81, 100; drug testing, 81; income, 102, 203n3 (chap. 5); marriage requirements, 103; youth views, 88–92 passim
Freedmen's Bureau, 32–33
Freire, Paulo: Pedagogy of the Oppressed, 82

Galton, Francis, 63–64
gangs, 110
gay, lesbian, and transgender people. See LGBTQ people
GED (General Education Development), 96, 103
The German Ideology (Marx and Engels), 180
Germany: Nazi era, 67
Gingrich, Newt, 23
Giuliani, Rudy, 131, 160
Global Women's Strike, 161
Gramsci, Antonio, 12, 153–55
"grandma revolt," Swedish, 163
Great Britain, 61
Great Depression, 38, 122
Greenberg, Gary, 82
Gregoire, Christine, 158
group homes. See foster care group homes
guardian ad litem, 135

Haitian children, adoption of, 41
Harlem, New York City, 45, 93, 137, 139
Harpers Ferry raid (1859), 32
Harris, Justin and Marsha, 104
Health and Human Services Department. See US Department of Health and Human Services
Hegle, Alise, 34–38 passim
Heritage Foundation, 23
Hessle, Sven, 163
Hispanic Americans. See Latinos
Hitler, Adolf, 67
HIV/AIDS, 44, 94
Holmes, Oliver Wendell, 66
homelessness, 6, 9, 13, 49, 79, 144; case studies, 2, 75, 93–97, 145–46; criminalization, 107
homeschooling, 104
homicide, 81
homophobia, 86–87
Hoover, J. Edgar, 109
hospitals, 60, 64, 68, 87; "sentinels" in, 6, 47. See also asylums and custodial hospitals
housing, 41, 44, 72, 121, 143; costs, 102; insecurity/instability, 6, 9, 79, 144. See also emergency housing; homelessness; supportive housing

Illinois, 84, 108, 145, 149, 152. See also Chicago
immigrants, 10, 19, 23, 65, 108, 170, 176; Sweden, 163. See also children of immigrants
immigration restrictions, 64
incarceration, 46, 114, 162, 166; of children, 19; of youth, 107–15 passim, 137
income: aged-out people, 84; agency CEOs, 100, 150; foster parents, 102. See also Supplemental Security Income (SSI); wages
Indiana, 65, 115
Indian Adoption Project, 53
Indian Child Welfare Act (ICWA), 53–54, 56, 57
Indians, American. See Native Americans
industrialization, 61–62, 107, 119, 171–72
inequality, 122, 156, 157
infants, newborn. See newborns
In re Gault, 109, 137
In re Nicholson, 137
In re Winship, 109, 136
"institutional defenders." See legal service organizations
institutionalization of "feeble-minded." See "feeble-minded," institutionalization of
institutional racism, 31–58 passim, 146
intellectual disabilities, 60, 62, 63, 67–73 passim, 138
international adoption, 41, 104
interracial marriage, 64, 177
involuntary sterilization. See sterilization: involuntary
Italian Socialist Federation, 21

jailing. See incarceration
Jewish organizations, 21, 104–5
Journal of Progressive Human Services (JPHS), 128
judges, 118, 135; corruption, 111–13 passim
Justice Department. See US Department of Justice
juvenile courts, 108, 109, 110, 112
"juvenile delinquency." See "delinquency" and "delinquent youth,"
juvenile justice system, 4, 107–15

Kansas, 148, 152
kickbacks. See bribery

"Kids for Cash" scandal. *See* Pennsylvania: "Kids for Cash" scandal
King County, Washington, 37
"kinship" foster care, 5, 101, 163
Kirshbaum, Hal and Megan, 73
Kollontai, Alexandra, 164, 183–87

labeling, 44, 60, 62, 65, 81–82; Sweden, 164. *See also* "deserving poor" and "undeserving poor"; psychiatric labeling
labor, 182; "reserve army" of, 172–73, 174. *See also* child labor; unemployment
labor market, 24–25, 33, 61–63 passim, 85–86, 121, 170, 174
labor power, 8, 51, 99
labor unions. *See* unions
Latinos, 45, 173, 198n19
Laughlin, Harry, 64
Lawrence, Massachusetts, Bread and Roses Strike (1912). *See* Bread and Roses Strike (1912)
lawsuits, 105, 112, 136–37
lawyers, 1, 5, 35, 95, 101, 111, 117, 135–38; collusion by, 66. *See also* public defenders
Lee, Tina, 44
Legal Aid Society, 105
legal service organizations, 105, 136, 137–38
leisure, 182
"lemon law" model (adoption), 148–49
LGBTQ people, 65, 67, 125, 128; Soviet Union, 186; youth, 11, 86–87, 93–97. *See also* transgender youth
The Life of the Street Rats (Brace), 20
Lipsky, Michael, 117–18
litigation. *See* lawsuits
locked-down facilities, 63, 93, 107–13 passim. *See also* incarceration
Los Angeles, 46–48 passim

Los Angeles County, 131–34 passim; Department of Children and Family Services (DCFS), 119, 134, 161; legal defenders, 136
Los Angeles Times, 132–33
Louisiana, 42, 82
Loving v. Virginia, 41
Luzerne County, Pennsylvania, 111–12, 152
Lynch, Jacqueline, 100

Malcolm X, 39–40
maltreatment of children. *See* child maltreatment
Marable, Manning, 39
marijuana, 103
marital status of parents. *See* unmarried mothers and fathers
marriage law, 64, 69, 177. *See also* divorce
marriage requirements, 103
Marx, Karl, 8, 51, 171, 179–83 passim; on pauperism, 173
Marxism, 169–71, 179–87 passim
Massachusetts, 68, 83; Department of Children and Families (DCF), 70–71. *See also* Bread and Roses Strike (1912)
Massachusetts Society for the Prevention of Cruelty to Children, 22
Master of Social Work (MSW) degree, 124
McGraw, Phil, 54
media, 6, 54, 118, 145; in "civil society," 12; panics and sensationalism, 109, 132–33, 145; welfare workers and, 118
Medicaid, 72, 81, 83, 85, 208n1
medication, prescription. *See* prescription drugs
mental health, 8, 80, 81. *See also* mental illness

mental health services, 5, 7, 10, 39, 79, 93, 146, 156; racism, 36; "sentinels" in, 47

mental illness, 10, 93, 94, 97, 115, 146

Meridian, Mississippi, 112

Metzenbaum, Howard, 41

Michigan, 83, 148

Minnesota, 52, 57, Red Lake Ojibwe, 115; State Bar Association, 165

Mississippi, 33, 112

moralism, 120, 175–76. *See also* blaming the victim; "sexual immorality" and "sexual deviance" (labels)

Mulally, Bob, 157, 162

Multi-Ethnic Placement Act (MEPA), 41, 42

Murray, Charles, 23–24

The Naked Communist (Skousen), 186

National Association of Black Social Workers (NABSW), 40, 124, 197–98n10

National Association of Social Workers (NASW), 124–25, 128–30

National Children's Law Conference, 158

National Incident Study of Abuse and Neglect (NIS), 47, 48

National Lawyers' Guild, 137

National Mentor, 149

National Welfare Rights Organization (NWRO), 124

Native Americans, 10, 52–58; adoption, 37; boarding schools, 23, 52, 55; foster care, 37, 52, 56, 57, 198n19; Minnesota, 115; South Dakota, 23; unemployment, 173

Nazi Germany. *See* Germany: Nazi era

Nebraska, 151, 152

neglect. *See* child neglect

newborns, 60

Newby, Dangerfield, 32

New York City, 42, 44, 45, 146, 162; anticommunism, 123; "Central Park Jogger," 114; child welfare statistics, 5; CWOP, 160–62; drop-in centers, 96, 97; foster care panic, 145–46; foster youth experiences, 88–97; Giuliani, 131, 160; "House of Refuge," 107; legal defenders, 136, 137–38; LGBTQ youth, 86–87, 93–97; Myls Dobson, 145–46; NASW chapter, 128; NY/NYIII, 94, 96; RASSW, 124; religion-based foster care, 104–5; SCO Family of Services, 81; unions, 123, 130–31; University Settlement House, 121. *See also* Children's Aid Society; Harlem, New York City

New York City, Administration for Children's Services (ACS), 1–4 passim, 26–30 passim, 81, 131, 145–46, 160.

New York City Division of Child Protection (DCP), 1–4 passim

New York City Housing Authority (NYCHA), 2, 4

New York Police Department, 1

New York State, 114; Andrew Cuomo, 129; Office for People with Developmental Disabilities (OPWDD), 71–72

Nicholson case. See *In re Nicholson*

NIS. *See* National Incident Study of Abuse and Neglect (NIS)

Nobody's Children (Bartholet), 48

"noncompliance." *See* "compliance" and "noncompliance," parental

nonprofits' excess revenue, 149–50

Norplant, 144

Nuremberg Laws, 67

NY/NYIII, 94, 96

objectification of children, 78, 82
Oliver, Michael, 61
*The Origin of the Family, Private
    Property and the State* (Engels),
    183
orphanages, 23, 24, 25, 31
orphans, 20, 21; Cuba, 165
"Orphan Trains," 20–23 passim, 33,
    49, 103, 119
Othello (literary figure), 50
"out-of-home care." *See* foster care

parents' rights, 69–70, 135, 161, 175,
    193–94. *See also* termination of
    parents' rights (TPR)
paternalism, 126, 127
Pedagogy of the Oppressed (Freire), 82
Pennsylvania: "Kids for Cash" scan-
    dal, 111–13. *See also* Philadelphia
People's Institute for Survival and
    Beyond, 128
People United for Children (PUC),
    114
pepper spraying of juvenile inmates,
    113
"performing compliance." *See* "com-
    pliance" and "noncompliance"
Perot, Ross, 144
Personal Responsibility and Work
    Opportunity Reconciliation Act
    (PRWORA), 24, 129
Pettigrew, Withelma "T" Ortiz
    Walker. *See* Walker Pettigrew,
    Withelma "T" Ortiz
Philadelphia, 144, 161
philanthropy. *See* private
    philanthropy
physical disabilities, 69, 73
Pius XI, Pope, 66
Piven, Frances Fox, 125–27
police, 4, 153, 174; data-driven
    management, 1; "hard" vs. "soft,"
    166; stop-and-frisk policies, 162
"political society" (Gramsci). *See*
    "coercive state" (Gramsci)

poorhouses, 19, 22
Pope Pius XI. *See* Pius XI, Pope
post-traumatic stress disorder, 80, 93
poverty, 101, 133, 140, 146, 154–59
    passim, 165, 166, 173–76 passim;
    disability and, 59; Marx on, 173.
    See also child poverty; "deserving
    poor" and "undeserving poor";
    poorhouses
Pratt, Richard, 52, 53
pregnancy, 63, 65–66, 68, 72, 84.
    See also abortion; sterilization
prescription drugs: psychotropic, 46,
    83–84, 93
The Principles of Communism
    (Engels), 180
prison. *See* incarceration
prisoners, sterilization of, 67
private detention centers. *See* for-
    profit detention centers
private philanthropy, 120, 158–59
private property, 182
privatization, 129, 147–52
professional child welfare workers.
    See child welfare professionals
Proposition 21 (2000), 110–11
prostitution, 63, 65, 181
pseudoscientific eugenics. *See*
    eugenics
psychiatric diagnoses: foster youth,
    93; parents, 60, 62, 63, 68, 69, 71
psychiatric institutions, 67, 93–97
    passim
psychiatric labeling, 46, 82, 127
psychology, adolescent and child,
    108, 120
psychotropic prescription drugs. *See*
    prescription drugs: psychotropic
PTSD. *See* post-traumatic stress
    disorder
public defenders, 75
public education, 52, 85, 121, 169
punishment, corporal. *See* corporal
    punishment

racialization, 49, 50, 107, 109
racism, 23, 24, 121, 157, 176, 177.
    See also backlash, racist; institu-
    tional racism; "Undoing Racism"
    projects
racketeering, 111–12
Radical Association of Social Ser-
    vice Workers (RASSW), 124–25
radicalism in social work, 122–28
    passim
Radical Social Work (Bailey and
    Brake), 125–27, 130
Rank-and-File movement (social
    work), 122, 130
rape, 65–66, 104, 114
"rehoming," 104
religion, 175. *See also* Christianity;
    foster care: religion-based
Represent: The Voice of Youth in Care:
    excerpts, 88–97
restorative justice programs and
    restitution, 115
Richmond, Mary, 120–21
Rise, 161; excerpts, 26–30, 34–38,
    55–58, 139–41
Roberts, Dorothy, 25, 47, 48,
    114–15; *Shattered Bonds*, 45–46
Roberts, Ed, 73
rural youth camps, 108
Russian Revolution, 164, 183

Salaam, Sharonne, 114
Salaam, Yusef, 114
scandal and scandals, 111–13, 131,
    134, 160
Scandinavia, 162–64
Scanlon, Michael, 22
scapegoats and scapegoating, 11, 42,
    133, 145, 156
schools, 33, 174; for "fee-
    ble-minded"; special education,
    46; "zero tolerance," 112. *See also*
    boarding schools
school-to-prison pipeline, 114
"scientific charity," 119–20

SCO Family of Services, 81
Scoppetta, Nicholas, 160
Seattle Children's Hospital, 68
Selivanoff, Shrounda, 34–38 passim
sentencing, 40–41. *See also*
    Drug Offenders Sentencing
    Alternatives
"sentinels," 47, 48
"serious emotional disturbance"
    (SED), 46
Service Employees International
    Union (SEIU), 131, 132
settlement house movement, 121–22
sex, teen, 109, 164. *See also* teen
    pregnancy
sex surgery, 68. *See also* sterilization
sex trafficking of children. *See* child
    sex trafficking
sexual abuse, 70, 79, 81, 125. *See*
    also rape
"sexual immorality" and "sexual
    deviance" (labels), 65
"sexually promiscuous" (label), 164
Shakespeare, William: *Othello*, 50
*Shattered Bonds: The Color of Foster
    Care* (Roberts), 45–46
Skousen, Cleon: *The Naked Commu-
    nist*, 186
slavery, 31, 32, 50, 51, 82; of wives,
    171–72
Smith, Sharon, 51, 172
social democracy, Swedish, 162–64
"social disablement" (Oliver and
    Barnes), 60–61
"socially unfit" (Swedish label), 164
social reproduction, 8, 51, 62–62,
    169–77, 187
Social Security, 93
Social Service Employees Union
    (SSEU), 130–31
Social Welfare Workers Movement
    (SWWM), 124
social workers, 117–34; caseloads,
    123, 132, 134, 139–41; strikes,
    131–32; Sweden, 163

"soft police," 166
Solis, Yaselin Serenity, 93–97
solitary confinement, 113, 115
South Dakota, 23
Soviet Union, 164, 183–87 passim
SSI. See Supplemental Security
    Income (SSI)
state, extended theory of. See
    "extended theory of the state"
    (Gramsci)
state bailouts of private agencies,
    148, 152
"status offenses," 109
sterilization, 144; involuntary, 59,
    64–69 passim, 164, 177; Sweden,
    163–64
stigmatization, 21, 120, 127, 147,
    165
"street-level bureaucracy" (Lipsky),
    117–18
strikes: social workers, 131–32, 133,
    134
substance abuse. See alcohol abuse
    (alcoholism); drug abuse/
    addiction
suicide, 113
Supplemental Security Income
    (SSI), 93
supportive housing, 95–97 passim
Supreme Court cases. See US
    Supreme Court cases
surplus value, 170, 172
Sweden, 162–64
Sylvia's Place, New York City,
    95–96, 97

Talent, Jim, 24
teen pregnancy, 84
teen sex. See sex, teen
termination of parental rights
    (TPR), 69–70, 135, 153, 154,
    175
Texas, 81, 83, 151
theft, 109, 110

Theses on Feuerbach (Marx and
    Engels), 180
Thorne, William, 55–58
Through the Looking Glass (TLG),
    73–76 passim
Timmons, Philneia, 26–30
Title IV-E funds, 58
transgender youth, 11, 87
transracial adoption, 40, 41–42, 53,
    124, 197–98n10
Trattner, Walter I., 119–20
"trial discharge," 5
Truth, Sojourner, 31–32
Tubman, Harriet, 32
Turner, Nat, 31

"undeserving poor" and "deserving
    poor." See "deserving poor" and
    "undeserving poor"
undocumented immigrants, 23, 162
"Undoing Racism" projects, 128,
    162
unemployment, 166, 173; aged-out
    youth, 84; Britain, 61; disability
    and, 59; Great Depression, 122;
    in NASW Code of Ethics, 129,
    130; and "undeserving poor," 21
unions, 121, 122–23, 129, 130–32,
    151, 152
United Office and Professional
    Workers of America (UOPWA),
    122–23
United Parcel Service (UPS), 158
United Public Workers of America
    (UPWA), 122–23
unmarried mothers and fathers, 24,
    42
US Congress: hearings, 77, 109, 123
US Department of Health and
    Human Services, 24, 70
US Department of Justice, 70, 112
use value, 170, 172
USSR. See Soviet Union
US Supreme Court cases, 41, 53–54,
    65–66, 67, 109, 135

Utah, 56–57

vagrancy, 19, 33
Vesey, Denmark, 31
victim blaming. *See* blaming the
    victim
Vinnerljung, Bo, 163
Virginia, 65–66, 67, 103
visual impairment, 60, 61
Vogel, Lise, 170, 173

wages, 171, 172, 203n3 (chap. 5),
    207–8n1
Walker Pettigrew, Withelma "T"
    Ortiz, 77–78
Wallace, Joseph, 145
Walmart, 207–8n1
war on drugs, 40, 44, 110, 157. *See
    also* drug arrests and convictions
Washington State, 36, 37–38, 56–57,
    68, 113, 158
"welfare mothers"/"welfare queens,"
    24, 42
"welfare reform" bills, 24, 129
Wexler, Richard, 133
Wilder v. Bernstein, 105
Williams, Eric, 50
Winnebago people, 53
Winship case. See *In re Winship*
Wisconsin, 6, 84
Wolf, Sherry, 86
Woman Patriots, 186
women's oppression, 171–72, 179,
    180, 183–84

xenophobia, 176, 177

youth camps. *See* rural youth camps

"zero tolerance" movement in
    schools. *See* schools: "zero
    tolerance"
Zhenotdel, 164, 184

ABOUT HAYMARKET BOOKS

Haymarket Books is a radical, independent, nonprofit book publisher based in Chicago.

Our mission is to publish books that contribute to struggles for social and economic justice. We strive to make our books a vibrant and organic part of social movements and the education and development of a critical, engaged, international left.

We take inspiration and courage from our namesakes, the Haymarket martyrs, who gave their lives fighting for a better world. Their 1886 struggle for the eight-hour day—which gave us May Day, the international workers' holiday—reminds workers around the world that ordinary people can organize and struggle for their own liberation. These struggles continue today across the globe—struggles against oppression, exploitation, poverty, and war.

Since our founding in 2001, Haymarket Books has published more than five hundred titles. Radically independent, we seek to drive a wedge into the risk-averse world of corporate book publishing. Our authors include Noam Chomsky, Arundhati Roy, Rebecca Solnit, Angela Y. Davis, Howard Zinn, Amy Goodman, Wallace Shawn, Mike Davis, Winona LaDuke, Ilan Pappé, Richard Wolff, Dave Zirin, Keeanga-Yamahtta Taylor, Nick Turse, Dahr Jamail, David Barsamian, Elizabeth Laird, Amira Hass, Mark Steel, Avi Lewis, Naomi Klein, and Neil Davidson. We are also the trade publishers of the acclaimed Historical Materialism Book Series and of Dispatch Books.

ALSO AVAILABLE FROM HAYMARKET BOOKS

101 Changemakers
Rebels and Radicals Who Changed US History
edited by Michele Bollinger and Dao X. Tran

Alexandra Kollontai
A Biography (Revised Edition)
Cathy Porter

Detroit: I Do Mind Dying
A Study in Urban Revolution
Dan Georgakas and Marvin Surkin

From #BlackLivesMatter to Black Liberation
Keeanga-Yamahtta Taylor

Marx on Gender and the Family
A Critical Study
Heather Brown

Women and Socialism (Revised and Updated Edition)
Class, Race, and Capital
Sharon Smith

ABOUT THE AUTHOR

Don Lash is an attorney and writer in New York City who spent ten years working within the child welfare system. As an attorney, he has specialized in disability, educational, and housing advocacy.